Conor McPherson was born in Dublin in 1971. He attended University College Dublin, where he began to write and direct. He co-founded The Fly by Night Theatre Co. which performed new plays in Dublin's fringe venues.

The Good Thief won a Stewart Parker Trust award in 1995. *This Lime Tree Bower* won a Thames TV award and a Guinness/ National Theatre Ingenuity award in 1996, and McPherson became Writer in Residence at the Bush Theatre, London.

A Selection of Other Titles in this Series

*Included in *The Crack in the Emerald: New Irish Drama*
selected and introduced by David Grant

Conor McPherson

THIS
LIME TREE
BOWER

Three Plays

Rum and Vodka
The Good Thief
This Lime Tree Bower

DUBLIN

NEW ISLAND BOOKS

LONDON

NICK HERN BOOKS
in association with the Bush Theatre

A Nick Hern Book/A New Island Book

This Lime Tree Bower, *Rum and Vodka* and *The Good Thief*
first published in Great Britain in 1996 as a paperback original
by Nick Hern Books, 14 Larden Road, London W3 7ST
in association with the Bush Theatre, Shepherd's Bush Green,
London W12 8QD, and in Ireland by New Island Books,
2 Brookside, Dundrum Road, Dublin 14

Front cover from design by Clodagh Noone

Typeset by Country Setting, Woodchurch, Kent TN26 3TB
Printed and bound in Great Britain by Athenaeum Press Ltd,
Gateshead, Tyne and Wear

New Island Books receives financial assistance from
The Arts Council (An Chomhairle Ealaion), Dublin, Ireland

A CIP catalogue record for this book is available
from the British Library

ISBN   1 85459 299 8 (Nick Hern Books)
       1 874597 43 X (New Island Books)

Author's Note

I think it's difficult for a writer to say much about their own work. But I have been in the fortunate position of directing productions of each of these plays and it's easier to say something about that.

The first problem for the actor performing these pieces is probably 'Where am I?' Where is the play set? I've made up my mind about this. These plays are set 'in a theatre'. Why mess about? The character is *on stage*, perfectly aware that he is talking to a group of people.

I've always tried to reflect that simplicity in productions. And what I have found out is that they work best when kept conversational, understated. That's what makes them believable. The temptation may be to launch into a one man 'performance', to 'act things out'. But such a performance will never be as interesting as one where the actor trusts the story to do the work.

That's what I've learned over the last few years. Keep it simple. The people who have helped me to learn this are the actors credited in this book.

I want to acknowledge the friendship and support of The Fly by Night Theatre Co. and I want to thank Philip Gray for his confidence in producing the premiere of *This Lime Tree Bower*.

RUM AND VODKA

For The Fly by Nights

Rum and Vodka was first performed at University College Dublin on 27 November 1992.

Performed by Stephen Walshe

Directed by Conor McPherson

It was subsequently performed at the City Arts Centre, Dublin, on 30 August 1994, by Fly by Night Theatre Company.

Performed by Jason Byrne

Directed by Colin O'Connor

Part One

I think my overall fucked-upness is my impatience.

I could never wait for anything to be over.

And I think that's the sign of an inquiring mind.

I don't want to do the investigations, I just want the answers.

And I reckon that because of that I'm a bit of a pessimist.

Because I never got any.

And that can lead to a lack of social graces.

I always feel that wherever I go, people look at me with a squinty face as if to say 'Now, just who the fuck are you?'

I think I hate the human race.

And I think they know it.

I often think the world gets together behind my back while I'm on the jacks or in bed and makes hasty decisions about new ways to get me to leave the planet.

They leave the meeting laughing.

Now, that's got to be the king of conspiracy theories.

But I know it's not true.

I suppose my impatience is due to my embarrassment a lot.

Maybe I don't like myself too much.

I hate looking back at things I've done.

So I'm always doing something new.

That means that my memories are like being different people.

But that's all a load of shit.

What I really want to tell you about is what's happened to me over the last three days.

I'm twenty-four going twenty-five.

I live on a new, well fairly new, estate in Raheny.

I'm married.

I have two young girls.

Until a couple of days ago I worked for the voting registration department of the corporation on Wellington Quay.

I'd been working there since I got married.

When I was twenty.

You might think that's quite young for someone to get married these days.

And I probably agree with you.

But em . . .

I had been going out with a girl since I was eighteen. We had been going out for two years.

And I mean, you're twenty.

What the fuck do you know? I mean, I was still trying the world for size.

Do you understand me? I was arsing about.

You know? I was messing.

With other girls.

I don't think I ever meant it to happen.

It usually happened when I had too much to drink.

But, ah . . . I was at this party one night and I ended up half comatose in the back garden.

And this girl, friend of a friend, decided she was going to look after me.

While I got sick in her shoe.

She stayed with me all night.

And I was grateful and I thought I felt something for her, and as the night wore on and everyone went home it was mostly horny.

I'm not going into the sordid details.

My life's one big sordid detail.

But we ended up being intimate.

On a number of occasions that night.

And I ended up seeing her for, well, whatever reasons after that.

And all the while I was still going out with my girlfriend and this other girl, the party girl, knew I was. Alright?

And then when the chewing gum lost its taste I stopped seeing her and decided to be faithful again.

For, well, forever.

But then I got a phone call from the party girl.

She was having a baby.

And now she's my wife.

You have to understand I didn't marry her for religious or moral . . . I mean, we didn't have to get married at all.

But as more and more people found out . . .

My mum and dad were furious.

My friends thought I was a fucking fool because they liked my girlfriend.

And my girlfriend.

Well I think it's the worst thing that ever happened to her in her life.

And . . . I have nothing else to say about that except that sometimes I . . . miss her.

So anyway.

There I was.

Lowest of the low, with no-one really to turn to except this pregnant girl.

And she was the only one who didn't criticise me.

We got on well enough and the more shit I got off other people the more I found comfort with her.

I ended up saying, 'Fuck you, everybody!'

Got a job, hundred and eighty quid a week, got a mortgage and figured my life finally had some direction.

And I got down to it.

I was the real nine to five animal.

And it was alright.

I spent the next two years getting on with making money, getting my wife pregnant again and drinking at the weekends.

The thrill of having your own house.

I could do what I liked.

I was a pretty good family man.

I remembered birthdays and I was Santa.

And the freedom.

I was always waiting for a knock at the door and a slap. But it wasn't going to come. I was grown up. I was allowed.

If I wanted to I could drink 'til three o'clock, watch videos 'til dawn, fuck my missus.

I mean, she was always there.

And that's one thing about that marriage.

Maybe there's never been too much . . . I don't know, but that's always been more than made up for in the bedroom.

Even from the outset.

We were married in a registry office.

There was very little ceremony.

But we spent our honeymoon in the house we were buying.

In Raheny.

And even though she was quite pregnant we got up to some of the weirdest stuff.

She's always been insatiable.

She often wakes me up with a cup of coffee which is like just an excuse.

She wants me there and then.

Even when she was huge with the baby she'd insist on doing it standing up with me behind her.

The complaints department weren't exactly run off their feet.

The kids came in a year of each other so we really had two babies in the house for a while.

I've never been gone on kids but I got a real kick out of these girls.

I know it's cruel, but I used to laugh at them trying to walk, falling on their arses or walking into chairs.

I thought that was very funny.

But as they got older I sort of felt like I was just playing at being Mr. Daddy.

And it all got a bit unreal. A bit hard to believe.

I still felt eighteen or sixteen.

And it came as quite a shock when I realised that this was as good as things were going to get.

I found myself ticking off the minutes at work, skiving in and out of flexitime, and, most importantly, drinking a lot.

This year especially it's got to the stage where I'm getting pissed every day.

The only days I don't drink are the ones where I'm too sick to move.

And it's this that really leads me on to the last three days.

Maria, my wife, and I've been fighting a lot recently.

She's been giving out about the money I'm spending, saving nothing, not coming in 'til one or two every morning.

Thing is, on top of everything, I'm an awful stupid bastard with money.

I don't drive and I jump in and out of taxis like there's no tomorrow.

I know it's ridiculous, but I don't know . . .

I'm just lazy . . .

I'm a thick fucker.

I tried cycling into work for a while.

I haven't cycled in years and Maria said it would keep me in shape as well as cutting down on expenses.

It worked for about three days.

I left the bike in the car park under work, but that meant it got locked in after six.

If I wanted to go for a few jars I'd have to lock it on the street somewhere.

I locked it to the railings of a house on Wellington Quay but then I decided to lock it inside the railings to make it harder to nick.

It worked because it was still there at half twelve that night.

Trouble was . . . my judgement was impaired.

When I unlocked it it fell right down into the basement.

All the lights in the house went on.

I ran down Wellington Quay because sometimes I'm shy.

I had no money for a taxi and I started walking, thinking I'd get the bike back in the morning.

I must have gotten some fright though, because only when I was half way up North Strand did I realise I was holding half a U-lock.

I think I'd have to say that my drinking or habitual drinking is due to two of the men I work with.

Phil Comesky and Declan Short.

They live together in a house in Killester which is the most disgraceful kip I've ever seen.

There's leftovers and remains of about a thousand takeaways, bottles, cans, socks, the place stinks.

It's a mixture of rotting and deodorant. They must spray the air.

I've ended up there hundreds of nights.

They drink, I mean drink, get drunk every day. They smoke about forty each as well.

They're both odd in their own ways.

Declan's got this girlfriend he's been going out with for about ten years.

They always fight. But you should see her drink. Pints. That's what keeps their flame aglow.

They fall around in each others' arms at closing time. Then they get two naggins. Vodka for him, Jameson or Powers for her, as long as it's Irish.

Every day. I'm serious.

Declan doesn't even have a beer belly.

He's one of those people who can drink a keg of Guinness, get four hours' sleep, and still look like he runs a health food shop.

I sometimes think that he'll be eating his breakfast one morning and it'll catch up with him. He'll disintegrate in seconds.

His girlfriend is a state though.

She looks like her mother shat her.

And that's pure drink.

Phil's the real spacer though.

He's been in and out of mental homes up 'til a few years ago.

When he was fourteen a boy on his road was killed when he was hit by a car.

It was a big tragedy at the time.

Big turnout at the funeral.

The boy who'd been killed had a girlfriend. They had been going out for about three weeks.

I mean. At that age.

She threw a letter into the grave when the coffin was being lowered.

And . . . she was young. She got over it.

She grew up.

Now, when Phil was twenty, no-one knows why, because he didn't even know the girl, he dug up the grave and got this letter out.

He broke into the girl's house at three o' clock in the morning, sat on her bed, and read it to her.

Nearly drove her mad.

I mean. That's real bonkers for you.

Anyway.

Last Friday lunchtime we were out having a drink.

We sank four pints each and I knew the weekend was going to be bananas.

I had been so depressed all week that to get paid meant get pissed.

Trouble was I was already hung over from the night before and my body was staging a coup.

I was finding it difficult to keep anything down.

All I wanted was to put my head on the desk and die.

I would have knocked off early saying I was sick, but there was some fuck up with the cheques and no-one was getting paid 'til four.

So I sat there sleepy and sick.

Bored stupid, wondering how I was going to get through the afternoon.

And everything went haywire.

Even now it's a blur.

Eamon Meaney, our arsehead of an office manager, came over to my desk in his Farah slacks and Clarke's shoes.

He used to be a national school teacher but he threw a tantrum one day and got fired. He was completely bald and thought he was gorgeous.

He had two queries with my work, and while I tried to dig myself out of a hole full of shit, I saw his expression change.

'Have you been drinking?' he asked me.

'I had a glass of wine with my lunch,' I slurred.

I must have smelled like a brewery, because he asked me just who I thought I was, getting drunk on tax payers' time and money.

I said I didn't know.

He told me to get into his office and walked off.

And I sat there.

Looking at the buildings on Batchelor's Walk, all falling down and filthy.

I saw the last name I had typed on my Apple Mac, Helen Falconer.

What a name.

Her ancestors must have been falconers.

Wow, I thought.

Meaney shouted across the room at me to hurry up.

Everyone looked at me.

People from every county.

I went red from my shoulders to my scalp and . . . I picked up my terminal, and I swung it out the window.

It sailed down two flights and right though the windscreen, and I didn't mean this, of Eamon Meaney's car.

Okay, I had a choice.

I could pretend to have a nervous breakdown and beg everyone's pity, or I could brazen it out.

'Do you have any idea how long I've wanted to do that for?'
I said.

They stared at me.

Meaney took a step backwards.

I picked up my jacket and strode out of the office.

As I went down the stairs I heard the door slam. I hadn't meant it but I was glad it did.

The day was overcast and people moved about on the street.

I went straight to The Norseman.

A pint and a short.

Never drank so fast.

Same again.

People in the pub.

Friday lunchtimers taking the afternoon off. Justified. They'd done their work.

And I felt so stupid and sick and guilty and angry and . . . low.

I wasn't very happy.

But I was glad of a drink.

It took the edge off my worries.

Brought out my self reliance.

If things are going well it helps you congratulate yourself.

If you're in the shitter it gives you all the righteous indignation of an innocent victim.

And by five o'clock I felt both.

At six Phil and Declan came in.

I was quite a sensation.

By seven we were discussing my future plans.

Fuck, the three of us'd go into business together.

We were going to be gardeners.

Out in nature and stuff.

No more fluorescent lights or instant coffee.

And oh yeah, no more drinking.

It was time to take our lives by the scruff said Phil and he got change for the cigarette machine.

We were mates said Declan.

I told the lads I loved them.

I told them I'd wanted to say that for a long time.

We all embraced and I went for a piss.

By ten the place was jammed.

None of us were talking much.

Just drinking.

I thought I was getting a temperature.

The floor swayed and I puked on the carpet.

We moved away from that spot and since the barmen hadn't seen, we got another one in.

By eleven I was nearly asleep.

The whole day felt like something that had happened to someone else.

I put my head in my hands and cried.

I cried until my eyes stung, 'til my gums felt swollen, 'til I couldn't lick my lips.

Then it was time to go.

Phil and Declan were arguing about economics. The argument went something like 'Fuck you.' 'No Fuck you.' 'That's bollocks.' 'You're a cunt.' 'Me?'

Like that. Like every fucking night.

Declan bought a bottle from behind the bar and we headed for the lads' house.

We had to stop the taxi for me to be sick and while I did, Phil ran up the road and got a Chinese.

Declan's girlfriend was back at the house with some friend of hers from Denmark.

I tried some whiskey but my throat was raw and I nearly got sick again.

Phil vanished upstairs with Miss Denmark and Declan and Siobhan crashed out on the couch.

I went outside. It was nearly two.

I walked along the Howth road to Raheny.

I turned left up Station Road and into my estate.

We live in at the back, in a cul-de-sac.

I went in quietly and took four paracetamol.

The lights were all out upstairs.

I undressed in the dark.

I was too tired to look for pyjamas.

I just slipped under the quilt and stayed as far over my side as possible.

I curled in a ball and shivered.

Maria moved close and held me.

I knew I was going to break her heart.

I'd always known it.

I wished I could wake her up and talk but I was too tired to think.

And then the curse of any tender moment, an erection.

I suddenly wanted her more than ever.

And drink'll do that to you.

And all this . . . aggression.

'This is my house.

I'm in bed with my wife.

And I'm going to fuck her now.'

I rolled over and felt her tits.

She was warm and soft.

I pulled the front of her nightie up and felt between her legs.

She was fast asleep.

I waited 'til she was ready, then I held myself above her like I was going to do press ups, and I slid inside her.

Suddenly it was bright.

It was morning.

The kids were shouting out the back.

I had a massive headache.

Like something was bursting out of my head.

My throat was sore and my mouth was so dry my tongue grated along the roof of my mouth when I unstuck it from my teeth.

And then I remembered . . .

Everything came flooding back and my stomach leapt.

This was very serious.

I could go to jail.

I needed a drink.

Fuck. Had I pulled out of Maria? Had she woken up to find me stuck up her? Did she have to push me off with disgust? I could hear her in the kitchen.

What was I going to say? I wanted to crawl under the quilt and hide like a kid.

I got up.

My clothes stank of smoke.

I put on Maria's dressing-gown and went down to the kitchen.

'Hi, hi.'

'You were late'

' . . . Yeah.'

She didn't seem any more annoyed than usual.

I must have pulled out.

I mean, that's pretty close to rape.

She'd have done her nut.

The kids saw me. 'Daddy, Daddy.'

I didn't know which was worse my headache or my guilt.

I couldn't take any tablets because Maria would start on at me about drinking.

I didn't want that.

What I was really worried about was how I was going to tell her I didn't think I had a job any more.

I ate a greasy fried egg I knew wasn't going to stay down, went upstairs, turned on the shower and puked into the toilet.

The shower was cold.

The immersion hadn't been on and I couldn't get a lather from the soap.

You see, this was a bit of a crisis because every Saturday we do the big shop.

We go down to Crazy Prices in Kilbarrack.

I knew I had about twenty-five quid in my jacket, but the messages usually come to about forty-five/fifty.

I was in trouble.

There was no way of not facing the music.

I had to tell her I'd no cheque.

But she was busy when I got dressed.

Getting the buggy ready, I don't know.

I was so tired.

I sat in the living-room and closed my eyes.

I had no idea how to go about this.

Then we were up and out.

Walking down the street.

Carol in my arms.

Niamh in the buggy.

Maria saying hello to people.

Up Raheny Hill.

Carol's hair on my face.

Into the car park.

It was starting to drizzle.

We got a trolley, Maria's list, and we were shopping.

I was forming mad plans.

I'm on a diet, I don't need food.

Let's have a severe economy drive.

But she'd know something was up.

And it was.

Something was up.

The trolley was filling up.

Maria was saying, 'Pampers, Pampers, toilet roll.'

I was pushing the trolley.

'Maria . . . '

'Yogurt, cheese . . . '

'Maria . . . '

'Mm?'

'Maria, I just remembered.

I never cashed the cheque, we got them late and I . . . '

'What . . . ?'

'I think I've lost my job.'

'What are you saying? Put that down Carol.'

'I threw my terminal out the window.

I'm so sorry.'

Maria went white.

She was puzzled.

She wanted this to be a joke but she knew it wasn't. And there was nothing I could do.

'I'm sorry.'

She hit me across the eye with a can of tuna.

I think I blacked out.

I tumbled backwards into a freezer with Bird's Eye fishfingers and pizzas and shit.

I could hear Maria screaming and she was thumping my legs and stomach.

People were watching.

The kids started crying.

I managed to crawl out the far side and stepped into someone's trolley.

They had left a child in the seat part and I toppled it over.

The child skidded across the floor and banged its head on a low shelf with raisins.

And I ran.

I ran down aisles of food and drink, past the cash desks, through the car park, through traffic lights, and down rows of houses past pubs.

I jumped on a bus and told the conductor town please.

The bus was packed with weekend shoppers.

I sat down beside a fat lady and knew I had to get pissed.

I went into the Flowing Tide on Abbey Street.

Pint and a short.

And a pint and a short.

Washing the burn of the whiskey away with beer.

My energy was coming back.

I wanted everything to just be okay.

If I could go back in time.

I've never felt so lonely.

I thought about ringing Phil and Declan, but I knew they were doing overtime, and there was no way I was ringing work.

No way.

Pint and a short.

Morning turned to afternoon.

I left to get a bite.

I was numb.

I crossed over by the Abbey down towards the quays.

An itinerant, a big man with short hair was being held on the ground by two guards.

He was crying.

He shouted at a woman 'Don't leave me here, you'll break my heart.'

She was going around the corner with a kid in a pram.

She stopped and shouted something back at him.

I didn't hear what it was but the man let his head fall on the pavement and his body was heaving with sobs.

He was a big man.

After seeing that I needed to get to the south side.

It's nicer.

I was starving.

I love tuna salad, like in a sandwich or a roll. Subs and Salads, South Anne Street.

Straight out of there into Kehoes nearby.

It was pretty full.

I was the only one on my own.

A man at the bar was telling his friends about Monopoly. Everyone goes round the board fifty times or whatever.

And you've made ten grand and you've made two. But look at the board, he said.

The odd hotel or house, but the board's still the same. Nothing's changed and people have made a fortune. What's been bought or sold?

He said it made you think about ownership.

What does it mean to own something?

Something you take for granted.

What does it mean, yours or mine?

It was making me think, so I split.

People tried to sell me stuff on Grafton Street, down Suffolk Street, across Dame Street and into Temple Bar.

I went down to The Norseman and I got lucky.

Phil and Declan had just arrived.

My eye must've been a bit red, they asked me what happened.

I didn't want to talk about it so when they asked how Maria took the news I wriggled out of it.

We got a round.

I found out that Meaney hadn't said anything.

He came to work with his car fixed, and the office window had been repaired that morning.

There was a new terminal on my desk.

We talked about how much better off I was without the job.

The three of us would go into business together. Have a delivery service, driving all around the country with the windows down. And on the continent we'd sleep in the trucks.

They wouldn't let me buy a drink and I suppose that was decent.

I had about ten quid to my name.

I wondered what Maria would do for money.

She probably had some put away.

She was bound to.

There'd be a dinner on the table.

I stopped worrying.

We had toasted sandwiches and plenty of pints.

The evening began to turn and the pub was filling up.

Declan said his girlfriend was in the Stag's Head and we decided to go up.

As we left The Norseman I had a terrible feeling which I can only describe as homesickness.

I suddenly wanted to play with the kids or have a bath with Maria sitting on the toilet talking to me.

I put it down to being drunk.

Get a few more pints inside me and I'd be happy as a pig in shit.

It was ten. Early days. Go home later. Give things a chance to settle for God's sake.

The Stag's Head was black.

People sat in the street drinking.

Declan's girlfriend was downstairs with her Danish friend.

They were wrecked.

We got some pints and everyone was having a laugh, but I just listened and smoked Phil's cigarettes.

I was looking at the punters.

Young people.

Students.

And then I saw this girl.

She was beautiful.

She had long hair past her shoulders.

Straight shiny brown.

I liked the way she was casual.

White sweater, leggings, pair of boots.

She was smoking and talking to some idiot.

He had glasses and was dressed completely in black.

He was all animated talking about a play he was writing about the IRA.

She was just smoking and looking at him.

I thought to myself, 'If I could be with that girl she could cure my life.'

I'd never have to worry about anything – what could go wrong?

At last orders I got a pint and a short.

The place was spinning.

I felt like I was in a big sleeping bag and I was looking at everything through a magnifying glass.

I wanted the lovely girl to look after me.

But I couldn't see her.

The Danish girl said she had tickets for us all to go and see Bjorn Again at midnight at the Olympia.

The barmen were kicking us out.

One of them shouted at me.

The others didn't notice.

I went upstairs to look for the girl, but she was gone.

I got sick in the street and waited for everyone.

I knew I couldn't go home in this state.

Two blokes asked me if I wanted hash.

I found I couldn't talk very well.

One of them gave me a dig and they started laughing.

I fell over and felt something wet.

It was where I'd been sick.

I think I lay there for a few minutes.

The next thing I remember is Phil picking me up and Declan saying, 'He needs a drink.'

I couldn't think or see straight.

Dame Street moved around my head.

I staggered along between the lads.

The Danish girl wiped my face.

I found it hard to keep my eyes open.

I got sick again and felt a little better. Phil told me I'd have to walk into the Olympia unsupported or none of us would get in.

I walked very slowly past the bouncers pretending to be listening to something Declan's girlfriend was saying.

For some reason I said 'Crane operator' and laughed but I can't remember what the joke was now.

The Danish girl handed over the tickets and we were in.

Our seats were upstairs.

The music hadn't started yet.

I fell into my seat and closed my eyes.

Then a cold drink in a paper cup was in my hand.

It was a concoction Declan claimed had power to wake the dead.

A rum and vodka with ice.

I took a gulp and a jolt shot through me.

I was sitting beside Miss Denmark.

Phil was kissing her.

He was licking her face.

One hand was up her skirt and the other one was on her tit.

A bouncer tapped Phil's shoulder and told him to cut it out.

He had to tell a lot of people.

Declan and Siobhan came back with another drink for me and said I looked a lot better.

Well I was awake.

Most of the people there were between thirty and forty.

Civil servanty types.

Nurses and guards.

Everybody was pissed.

People fell down the stairs or got sick in their seats.

There were a lot of really camp people too.

They spoke loudly and laughed at people they pointed out to each other.

A voice announced that the show involved a strobe light as a warning to people who who took fits.

A man in a yellow tee shirt shouted 'I'm an epileptic, I'm an epileptic.' And everybody laughed.

I didn't think it was very funny.

Bjorn Again came out and sounded exactly like Abba. They looked like them and moved like them. It was uncanny.

It was good for about half an hour but the joke wore off and it got boring.

I wandered off to the bar.

I found I still couldn't walk very well – it was hard to keep my balance.

Everything looked like it was on telly.

There was a group of young people down at the front dancing around and having a really good time.

Would they think I was one of the stupid fuckers falling around in my Argyll sweater? Feeling my fat girlfriend's tits in front of everybody?

Didn't they see that I was different?

I wanted to go down on the stage, grab a microphone and scream at everyone that none of what was happening to me was my fault.

I could've done a lot with myself.

I'm an intelligent bloke.

But of course, I didn't.

I got a rum and vodka at the bar after pushing about for ten minutes with housewives and queers.

In the confusion I managed not to pay.

The bar was jammed.

People paying in to drink.

But they had money to burn.

Fat bastards.

And then I saw the girl from the Stag's Head. A man about thirty-five, thirty-six was talking very earnestly to her.

Every now and then she'd smile and shake her head. The man took a step backwards and held out his arms like he wanted her to search him or something.

I leaned against the wall and had a smoke.

I was watching her.

She was gorgeous.

Her skin was really clear, and when she smiled there were creases beside her eyes making her look a lot older.

I figured her for about nineteen or twenty.

Her eyes were wide set.

Not like she was a mutant or anything.

Just, I can't describe people.

You could see her eyes.

My heart was thumping.

I gulped my drink and moved closer to hear what they were saying.

And when I heard her speak I knew she was the girl for me.

She was experienced, worldly, she could look after me.

The man was talking about his missus.

She was screwing his neighbour.

So it was nothing personal.

He just wanted to get even.

In his own head.

I winced and the girl saw me and smiled.

She smiled at me.

He went on and on.

They could get a hotel room, have a meal.

I made a face. 'Is this guy for real?'

She smiled at me again.

Because she was smiling the bloke thought he had a chance.

She could have a nice breakfast in bed.

A jacuzzi, and come on, he wasn't that bad looking was he? She smiled at me again, then she walked over and held my hand.

She was holding my hand.

The bloke said something about the place being full of lesbians and went back to the bar.

She looked at me and said thanks.

Then she made to go back to the show, but I held her hand and tried speaking to her.

'What?' she was saying, 'what?'

'Cure my life,' I said.

'I want you to cure my life.'

'I think you're beautiful.'

I burst into tears and everyone was looking at me.

She dragged me out of the bar and down to the girls' toilets.

There were some women in there doing their hair and make-up or whatever.

I told them to fuck off before they could tell me I was in the wrong jacks.

We went into a cubicle and she asked me if I was alright.

I couldn't stop crying.

I felt too sorry for myself and I was enjoying it too much.

Poor me . . .

I grabbed her and she gave me a hug.

And inside my head a little voice said, 'Hello . . . nice tits.'

She was asking me what the matter was but I was beginning to feel more horny than upset.

'I'm okay,' I said.

She said we should really get out of there.

Outside we met some of her friends.

Few guys, few girls.

The blokes looked like Bohemian film producers, the girls looked like a bunch of monkeys hooked on crack.

These people were very intense.

Even when they were trying to be funny.

But while she was talking to them she kept holding my hand.

I wasn't feeling horny then.

Just comfortable.

This was all very exciting.

We dumped the losers.

She wanted to know what the matter was but I just asked if we could go.

She didn't say anything.

She just led me down to where her coat was.

Her pals looked at me when she said she was off.

I gave them a moody scowl.

Couldn't they see there was a silent bond, a communication beyond words going on here?

Cunts.

We left the Olympia.

On the way out she squeezed my hand and smiled at me.

She was curing my life.

She hailed a taxi and I bundled in the back.

. . . Yes . . . she got in beside me.

. . . Okay.

She gave the guy an address.

I asked her where she lived.

She said Clontarf.

She lived with her parents but they were away.

'Is that where I'm going?' I asked her.

'Is that where you want to go?' she said.

I put my arm around her and she snuggled into me.

She was slender.

We sped through town.

People tried to flag our taxi.

I saw fights.

Men and women fighting.

Arguments outside chippers.

Drunks asleep in the street.

Down North Strand.

People walking home.

It was starting to rain.

And I was safe in the taxi with the woman I loved.

Through Fairview.

Along the coast.

The tide was out.

Rubbish all along the shore.

Now it was lashing.

I was nice and warm.

We turned left up by Clontarf Castle.

And stopped outside a huge house.

'That's six pounds seven.' The girl paid.

She helped me out of the car.

The front door was a huge slab of oak.

A dark house, smelled musty.

Smelled like the sea.

We were in the sitting-room.

Two plush green suites.

Carpets thick as your finger.

Patio doors lead to a wide garden. Everything was quiet.

She asked me if I wanted a drink.

A big rum and vodka, with lots of ice.

She had a beer.

We sat there smoking in the lamplight.

'What am I doing here?' I asked her.

'What do you want to do?' she said.

She took my hand and led me upstairs.

A square open landing.

Her door, a room at the back.

A big bed, a table full of books.

Wooden varnished floor.

Her own bathroom en suite.

I asked if I could take a shower.

She said of course.

I locked the door and took a big shit.

I turned on the shower and undressed.

My feet on the tiles.

I saw myself in the mirror.

I looked like I was dead.

Like I'd been beaten to death.

I scrubbed myself from top to bottom.

I was pissed out of my head.

I felt okay.

I dried myself with a nice towel.

My clothes were manky.

I put on her robe and went into the bedroom.

She was in bed.

I was trembling all over.

'You getting in?' she asked me.

I shut the bathroom door and took off the robe.

She pulled back the quilt and I climbed in.

The bed was warm.

She lay on top of me and started kissing my neck.

It was too late now.

My willy went boing.

She laughed and grabbed it.

'What's your name?' I asked her.

'Myfanwy', she said, 'It's Welsh.'

End of Part One.

Part Two

The first thing I remember about waking up is that horrible feeling like you're falling off a cliff.

Everything came flooding back like a kick in the bollocks.

I was lying in a room that shouted money, in bed with a rich girl called Myfanwy.

I checked her bedside clock.

Quarter to ten.

Twelve hours ago I was thinking about going home.

What had happened? The sun was blazing through the window.

Myfanwy was asleep with her back to me.

I could barely remember what she looked like.

I thought about what a slut she was taking a complete stranger to her bed.

The more I thought about it the more disgusted I was.

I'm a married man.

Even if she had no respect for me, at least she should have thought about my wife.

I dozed, and when I looked at the clock again it was eleven.

My head was exploding.

I needed some painkillers or a drink, or both.

My clothes were on the bathroom floor.

I put on her robe and took my stuff downstairs to the washing machine.

I threw everything in except my shoes.

I'm not even going to try describing what kind of shape I was in.

Every movement was an effort.

I found some paracetamol and opened a beer.

Our glasses were where we had left them in the sitting room.

I sat there in someone else's house drinking their beer.

There were photographs on the walls.

Weddings, graduations, black and whites.

I felt like an intruder.

I looked at their videos and their C.D.'s.

I tried playing their piano.

I lay under their coffee table.

They never could have guessed that all the stuff they took for granted would ever receive this much attention.

I was still drunk.

Maria would think I stayed in Phil and Declan's.

I could go home and make it up to her.

I didn't quite know how, but I would.

I was going to sacrifice all my free time and show her I was sorry.

But what was I sorry for? I couldn't go back to my job.

I just couldn't.

She was the one who hit me in Crazy Prices.

I don't think I deserved that.

I didn't know what to do.

I went upstairs.

Myfanwy was still asleep.

I wanted to get out.

I wished I hadn't put my clothes in the machine.

I could've split.

There was a pair of pink tracksuit bottoms on the back of a chair.

I put them on and got a pair of tiny socks out of a drawer.

I found a tee shirt and got my shoes.

The sun was baking down.

I left the door on the latch, and strolled up the road.

I went around by the Cricket club and down Belgrove Road as far as Vernon Avenue.

Then I turned right.

Down to the seafront.

Clontarf is beautiful.

Old houses and trees, the breeze comes over the sea, and there's a ghost on every corner.

People were coming and going to mass.

I went down the coast and into the Dollymount house.

It was huge. A boozerama.

I got a pint and a short and sat at a window looking at the bay curving round to Howth.

You could see everything clearly.

It was peaceful.

I wished I was on top of Howth Head, looking at Dublin.

I wished it was a couple of years ago and I was making plans instead of just drifting with whatever went on.

I had another pint and it made a huge difference.

I felt much better.

I had about four quid to my name.

I knew I wanted to get pissed before holy hour so I mooched back along the coast to Myfanwy's road.

I heard a radio in the kitchen when I pushed the big front door open.

'Is that you?' she shouted.

'Yeah.' I said, because I'm witty like that.

She bounded to the kitchen door and looked out at me.

She started laughing and told me my clothes would be ready soon.

She asked me if I was hungry.

I said a sandwich would be fine.

We sat in the kitchen for a while.

She gave me a can of beer and asked me where I'd gone.

When I told her she said I drink too much. She wanted to know who was playing the piano at the crack of dawn.

I said it wasn't me, and she said no, it was nice.

She started asking me about myself.

She didn't even know my name.

I said it was Michael.

She wanted to know where I lived and worked.

I couldn't answer her.

I knew she had her suspicions, but I'm a coward and I asked her questions instead.

She'd been a student at Trinity.

She had a degree in Italian and something else.

She was going to do a business diploma.

I asked her if she had a hangover.

She said she hadn't been drinking.

For some reason I found that perverse.

I told her I wanted to go into town.

She gave my clothes a shot in the drier.

I had another beer and ate my sandwich.

I didn't feel like talking much.

She sat on my lap and started kissing me but I didn't feel much like that either.

She said I'd changed my tune since last night, and did I not think she was beautiful any more?

Of course, talking about last night she might as well have been talking about the Boer War as far as I held myself responsible.

I told her I was tired and maybe later.

But her parents were coming home later she said.

I know this seems shitty, but if I was going to get pissed I had to stay on her good side and time was ticking away.

I spent half an hour banging her on the sitting-room floor.

Then she ironed my pants and I was going mad because it was half one.

We'd never make it in time.

She laughed and said we'd take her car.

She had a fucking car.

She turned on the alarm and took her mini out of the garage.

Zoom.

She was a pretty good driver.

We were sitting in Davy Byrne's (her choice) at ten to two.

We both had pints.

Then I had a pint and a short.

Then I had another pint and Myfanwy had a glass. She paid. She knew.

We were finally kicked out at half two.

That felt much better.

And only another hour and a half 'til the next one.

Myfanwy asked if I was okay.

'Oh yeah, fine.'

She asked what I wanted to do now.

I didn't mind.

We walked around for a while.

Around Merrion Square and St. Stephen's Green.

She asked me questions.

At the start when I wouldn't answer she thought it was sort of fun, but I could see it was beginning to annoy her now.

She was bored with the mystery man.

I felt rotten about it.

We sat down in a place on South Anne Street for something to eat.

I told her everything that had happened over the last two days.

She was excited.

She liked me.

I impressed her.

She didn't mind that I was married or anything.

I told her about my daughters.

But then I had to stop.

It was none of her fucking business.

She wanted to know if there was anything she could do.

I said, 'No . . . just keep paying.'

She laughed and put her arms around me. After she had held on to me for a minute she looked at me but although she was smiling she was a bit tearful for some reason.

I suppose it was a bit sad.

It was still very warm so we took our coffee outside.

We sat at a table like garden furniture and she said she thought I should ring my wife.

But I was too embarrassed and guilty.

She wanted to know if she could see me again. I didn't know.

Anyway she said, we had the rest of the day.

There was a party in Rathmines that night and would I go.

Of course, I said I would.

Anything to avoid thinking about going home just yet.

Then a group of Myfanwy's friends came along.

Everybody wanted to hug Myfanwy.

I think they reckoned I was just someone sitting at her table.

They seemed a bit surprised when she introduced me.

There was Rupert, a huge bloke who looked like an officer in the SS.

Feargal, a squatty little guy with glasses that had a cord going round the back of his neck.

Sorcha, who looked like a model.

Jane, who had a complexion like dark cream.

And Sinead who spoke Irish as much as she could.

They all got coffee.

My buzz was wearing off but Myfanwy seemed to want to stay there.

Rupert was at acting school.

His class were doing a modern version of King Oedipus and everybody had to go.

He had learned so much about himself since the start of rehearsals.

There's nothing in modern drama that isn't in Greek tragedy and comedy.

I asked him what the theatre had to do with real life.

I thought he'd have an answer seeing as he was at a school and everything.

But he went on for about ten minutes and it was very boring.

I can't remember what he said.

Then he started to explain why comedy is funny breaking it down into some Russian cunt's three 'levels' of humour.

No-one laughed.

He kept touching Myfanwy's hand.

I wanted for me and her to go and get sloshed.

Sorcha was a model.

She had done an ad for shampoo where no-one saw her face, just the back of her head.

Then a fight broke out when Feargal said he thought Christy Turlington looked like a baboon.

They talked about Rwanda.

Friends of theirs abroad.

A girl they knew was pregnant.

A lecturer at Trinity who wore pink cords.

They spoke about how the country would never forgive Dick Spring for going into government with Albert.

And I wanted a pint.

I knew I was as intelligent as these fuckers.

But I just didn't seem to have any opinions.

I was embarrassed sitting there.

I eventually got the nerve to ask Myfanwy to come for a drink.

To my dismay, everyone thought this was a great idea.

We went to the International Bar.

Going down Grafton Street and Wicklow Street Myfanwy held my hand.

I was shitting someone I knew would see me.

I wasn't enjoying myself.

I sat back in the pub and let Myfanwy do the buying.

She did the necessary.

She was curing my life.

Her friends drank a pint an hour.

Myfanwy and I drank steadily.

Pace is the secret.

I was feeling a little better.

I was talking to Jane, the girl with the complexion like dark cream.

I told her a joke about niggers and she lost the head.

I didn't talk to her again.

And then Feargal and her left to collect Feargal's kid from his ex-girlfriend.

I asked Sorcha if being a model meant people treated her like a bimbo, or a good-looking object.

She said no and I didn't pursue it.

I was bored.

Myfanwy got me a rum and vodka.

Rupert told us about a film script he was writing with a friend of his from college.

It was about a girl who wants to be an artist but lacks the confidence.

He wanted to set it in Paris and have it done in French.

It would be more beautiful.

I asked if he spoke French.

He said not really but it was going to be subtitled.

I didn't understand, but he'd had three pints so I let it go.

He told us he found women more interesting than men.

He wanted to be a woman.

He wasn't gay or anything.

He just thought women have better insights and if they ran things the world wouldn't be as fucked up.

I told him I thought he was a prick.

But Myfanwy laughed and the others thought it was a joke.

It turned out to be Rupert's party we were going to.

They left for his house to get things ready.

It was dusk and the pub was nearly empty.

Myfanwy put her head on my shoulder and told me she didn't know what to say.

I told her that was alright, because I wasn't interested anyway.

She laughed and held me.

Then we got up and went out to her mini.

We stopped on George Street and Myfanwy gave me a fiver to get fags.

I bought two packs.

Camel lights and Gauloises.

I was being a classy guy I explained to Myfanwy.

'Mmm . . . ' she said, 'Mind if we take a detour?'

We drove to Ranelagh and stopped outside a house Myfanwy said was her brother's.

She was going to dress me properly.

Her brother was in Pakistan writing a history textbook.

We went up to his bedroom.

She opened the huge wardrobe and started throwing things onto the bed.

Hundreds of pounds' worth of shirts.

A jacket that cost five hundred pounds.

A tie that cost seventy pounds.

And that's what I'm wearing now.

I don't think it does much for me but it felt classy at the time.

While I was standing there half undressed Myfanwy started feeling me up.

I knew what I had to do and I did it.

We were back in the car at ten.

I took a bottle of vodka from her brother's drink cabinet.

We could hear the music coming from Rupert's house from down the road where we were parked.

He had the house to himself and there were people in every window.

We walked in past people drinking in the garden.

A couple were snogging in the hall.

We went into the kitchen.

Myfanwy was talking to some friends of hers in the doorway.

I sat at the kitchen table and poured some vodka into a mug.

A bunch of lads from the country asked for a sup.

I passed them the bottle and they slugged out of it.

Some blokes over at the back door kept going out for a joint.

I don't think they were afraid of being caught, they just didn't want to share it.

Another bloke was standing at the cooker making himself some soup.

A girl stood behind him with her hands in his front pockets.

Two girls and a bloke stood in front of me at the table talking about films I'd never heard of.

I went to have a look around.

The music was all techno.

There were people in the living-room going mad to it.

MTV was on with the sound down.

Myfanwy was dancing.

She looked fabulous.

She had a sleeveless check shirt and a pair of shorts.

Rupert was dancing like he'd just been let out of a mental home.

A young couple sat on the floor in a corner.

They were having a shit time.

The girl made half-arsed attempts to get her boyfriend up to dance but you could see neither of them really wanted to.

I sat down with them and we shared the bottle.

The girl took a smoke.

I wanted to know what was wrong with them.

I wanted them to relax and cheer up. It sort of became important to me.

They kept saying they were alright but I knew they were fucked.

What was it about them?

I don't know.

'I hope it'll be okay,' I said.

'That's all I'm going to say to you.'

I went to pour them more drink but the bottle was gone.

We looked around.

Someone had taken it.

Then the girl saw it.

The muckers from the country had it.

They were sitting on the couch talking to a very beautiful girl.

If they had asked I would've given them some.

The girl said she was going to ask them to give it back.

'No,' I said, 'Don't ask.'

I stood up and bent over the couple. I shook the guy's hand and kissed the girl on her forehead.

I was a bit upset.

I went over to the couch.

The muckers looked at me.

One of them had the bottle between his legs trying to hide it.

I grabbed it away from him and swung it at his face.

The bottom of it hit his nose right on the bridge.

That really fucked up his face.

The bottle hadn't smashed so I heaved it against the side of another bloke's head.

It broke with a pop and glass went everywhere.

Someone screamed.

I went to find Myfanwy.

We were going.

She wasn't in the kitchen or out the back.

She wasn't on the stairs or in the toilet.

There was no-one in the first bedroom. A pair of eejits were playing guitars in the next one.

The lights were off in the third.

Bad news.

I found the switch.

Myfanwy was on the bed.

Her shirt was open and her shorts were around her feet.

Rupert's head was between her legs.

He was kneeling on the floor pulling himself off.

The first thought that went through my head was 'He's licking my spunk.'

Myfanwy saw me and started kicking him away.

But he kept a hold of her.

I started laughing.

He lifted his head up and said 'Squeeze your tits, I'm coming.'

He saw me and came.

Myfanwy rolled over and put her head in her hands.

Rupert pulled the quilt off the bed and covered himself.

'Goodbye.' I said.

The lights were all on downstairs and the music had stopped.

People brought towels in and out of the living-room.

I saw Myfanwy's jacket on a chair beside the hall phone.

I took her wallet and left.

The night was warm.

Myfanwy had twenty quid.

I hailed a taxi and said, 'Raheny please'.

'You were walking the wrong way mate,' he said.

We drove through town, through Fairview, up the Howth road, across Sibyl Hill and into Raheny village.

'This is fine,' I said.

I was hungry so I went over to the chipper.

It was about twelve o clock and the chipper was packed.

There were two men in front of me who were about forty.

They were wrecked.

One of them had a little girl with him who was about two.

She was sleepy and crying.

He was asking her if she wanted chips.

Then he told his friend he was dead.

His missus would kill him.

I didn't feel hungry after that.

I made my way back to the estate.

One or two people were walking back from the pub.

All the houses the same.

Each one with a mortgage.

Each one with a love story.

I opened the front door quietly and crept upstairs.

Everything was like a tomb.

I went into my daughters.

I sat on the floor and listened to them breathing.

Their fair hair and white cotton pyjamas.

Their little hands.

I couldn't bear it.

THE GOOD THIEF

For Kevin Hely and Gina

The Good Thief was first performed under the title *The Light of Jesus* at the City Arts Centre, Dublin, on 18 April 1994 by Fly by Night Theatre Company.

Performed by Kevin Hely

Slide photography by Paul Kinsella

Directed by Conor McPherson

It was subsequently performed as part of the Dublin Theatre Festival on 4 October 1994, a Loopline production.

Performed by Garrett Keogh

Slide photography by Robbie Ryan

Designed by Anne Layde

Directed by Conor McPherson

Let's begin with an incident.

I was sitting in Joe Murray's bar one night, as I usually did.

I was talking to this couple I liked and having a few beers.

I was working for Joe Murray at this time as a paid thug.

I scared people for him.

Set fire to places.

Shot people. As warnings.

My girlfriend Greta had just left me but I still saw her most days because she had left me for Joe Murray.

Power attracts women.

Also, I had been beating her up and I knew it was wrong but I'm not the issue here, so let's leave it.

Let's not. She annoyed me.

She gave herself to any man who wanted it. I knew this for a fact and I was sick of sticking it where someone else had had it a few hours ago.

Anyway, I was having a few glasses of beer with this couple I really liked and relaxing.

That day I'd had to chase a man up and down his premises in Capel Street.

He knew all these stairwells and stuff you wouldn't think were there.

I was exhausted.

He was a shoe repair man.

I hate people with skills who can do stuff.

It's a small quibble but I refuse to constrain my personality.

I believe that that can lead to problems.

I must've broken every bone in his hands.

Then I shaved his head and kicked his nuts so many times he passed out.

This couple I was talking to were young and funny.

They came in and out sometimes.

They were friendly with each other too.

I was a little bit jealous of them but I was happy for them at the same time.

I was just having a few glasses of beer and we were chatting about politics and movies and the weather and stuff.

I saw Greta over the other side of the bar talking to Harry Delaney, a man who'd been living in England for a number of years and wore a necklace.

I felt like tossing my drink over at them but I was in too good a mood.

The couple I was talking to bought me a drink and I bought them one and we were talking about clothes and style.

Greta walked past me and didn't look.

She had her coat on and she was smoking.

I saw Harry Delaney shoot back his drink and go the long way round.

I knew what they were doing.

I was going mad but 'Fuck them,' I thought.

It was a cold night.

They'd have to do it in the car park.

They'd freeze their bare arses off.

And Greta would have to be back at closing time to suck Joe Murray's dick. Or whatever it was she did after hours.

I'm probably not being very fair.

But life's not fair.

So she was gone out with Harry Delaney and she was gone a few minutes.

I was shooting the breeze with this young couple I really liked and Joe Murray comes downstairs and starts looking around.

The look on his face made my day.

When he saw that Greta wasn't there he looked miserable and annoyed at the same time.

You see, I knew he loved Greta.

He was the type of man who would've put her in a china cabinet and polish her if he could.

But I knew what he liked.

He liked putting it up girls' arses and I'd seen him do it.

He was a right degenerate.

This was one of the things annoyed me about him and Greta. She probably enjoyed it. I always preferred it straight.

I'm not a messer.

He was looking around and people were talking to him. Asking him for favours or spoofing him he'd lost weight.

Eventually I heard him ask somebody where Greta was, but no-one had seen her go out.

He came around to us and I introduced everyone. The young couple were leaving.

I said I'd see them again and it was nice talking to them.

Murray bought me a drink and began talking a bit of business.

But I knew he was going to talk to me about Greta.

He had never squared it with me, the way she'd moved out of our place and into his.

I knew that if he mentioned it, it would annoy me too much.

He asked me had I seen her.

I said I had but I didn't know where she was.

Then it was sort of funny.

He said, 'Does she do this much? I mean go off without saying anything?'

I thought it was gas. Him asking me this.

It was very bad manners but I answered him anyway and said I didn't know.

I could see he knew he shouldn't have asked me for advice after taking her away from me. But sometimes he was as thick as shit. He really was.

Yeah.

Well. That's the incident I wanted to begin with. It's sort of funny, isn't it? Kind of sick as well.

There's just something not quite right about it. Hard to put your finger on though.

Anyway, something about it changed the way I felt about Joe Murray and the way I felt probably contributed to the mayhem that happened over the next few days.

And that's what I really want to talk about.

So that night I had a couple of beers after closing with Joe Murray and Vinnie Rourke, an old time vicious bastard who'd done fifteen years for armed robbery.

I didn't speak to him much and I'd heard he had 'mellowed with age'.

But I knew he was a psycho and that he did odd jobs for Murray when he wanted a real pro and not a messy bastard like me.

Greta came back and Murray was asking her where she'd been and where Harry Delaney was. But she didn't answer him. She just poured herself a big tequila and lit a cigarette.

Vinnie Rourke and a little fucker who followed him everywhere, Seamus Parker, were looking at her like they wanted to give her one each. Or at the same time.

Joe Murray always seemed weak when Greta was around.

I was imagining Murray doing it to her and her loving it. It disgusted me but I couldn't get it out of my head.

I had to bang a couple of shorts away.

I was messing with the jukebox, putting the Beatles on.

Murray came over and gave me a piece of paper with an address on it. It was a man called Mitchell who owned a number of warehouses which he leased to food importers mostly. But we also knew that from time to time he'd hold on to dodgy gear from some of the bigger robberies in the city. Antiques and that.

Murray had been threatening to set fire to Mitchell's warehouses for years.

This brought in about a grand and a half a month, but with the recession Mitchell was asking for some leeway.

Murray had refused and Mitchell was giving it all this guff about some second cousin in the IRA getting on to it.

My job was to go round to his house and scare him.

I told Murray okay and he gave me a hundred as a sub.

Back at the bar, Vinnie Rourke was staring at me. I knew that he didn't like Murray giving me work for some reason.

But I did my best to ignore him and put plenty of effort into drinking Greta out of my head.

It got hazy after that and I just remember driving home wishing I was more drunk.

When I woke up it was about nine and I had a blinder of a hangover.

I considered not doing the job for Murray but he had given me a sub and that meant it was important to him.

I did a trick from my days as a second lieutenant which always fooled my body into action.

First I took some aspirin and then some Vivioptal tablets which are a tonic, giving you energy after you've been sick, then a valium, and then I put the kettle on.

I ran a cold bath while I shaved, then I stripped and hitting the water was like being born. Everything went mad. I put my head under the water and blew bubbles.

Then I stood up and let my body get warm before sliding under for another shock.

I was shivering while I dried myself.

I made a huge hot whiskey with lemon and cloves and it blew the roof off my head.

Made me drunk very quickly.

I had another one and then I checked my guns.

The shotgun I had was beautifully hand-made by a man in Mullingar, but of course I'd ruined it by sawing the barrel in half.

It was lethal and it often frightened me to carry it. I was always worried it would go off.

I also had a very old, very beautiful Webley revolver which was more just in case. I was told that this one I had was used to give the coup de grâce to deserters in France. I never knew if that was true.

It was accurate up to about sixty yards and it was so pristine I doubted it had ever seen action.

It was starting to rain as I got into the car. I wanted to get this over with quickly before my hangover caught up with me.

There was only old tat on the radio but I kept it on for company.

When I was nearly there I took my bag of gear out.

I had a balaclava for extra frighteners and an industrial anorak because only mentlers wear them as everyday jackets.

The address I wanted was in a new estate where everything looked a bit pokey.

Looking back, I don't know why I put a cartridge in the shotgun.

My revolver was always loaded and I had it in the back of my jeans.

But I never trusted the shotgun.

I had very few cartridges anyway.

Maybe I wanted to make some noise if this Mitchell guy knew how how to take care of himself.

I'll never know, but it was one of the luckiest things I ever did.

I pulled on the balaclava and put the shotgun inside my jacket.

I thought I saw a curtain move upstairs but I wasn't sure.

I was ringing for about a minute when the door opened.

And there was a bloke in a balaclava.

He hit me in the face with a heavy cosh and grabbed my arm as I went for the shotgun.

He pulled me into the hall and kicked me on the back of the head.

I lay trying to get a grip on the radiator.

He slammed the door.

I heard a gun bolt and somebody said, 'Don't move.'

I froze.

My balaclava was pulled off and I was turned around.

My shotgun was on the hall table.

The man who'd grabbed me was standing in front of me and there was another one in overalls on the stairs holding an automatic rifle.

I knew this was out of my league and I was terrified.

I could see into the kitchen. Mitchell, who I was supposed to be scaring, was there with his wife and a little girl of about three or four.

Well, they were scared anyway.

The man on the stairs asked if Joe Murray had sent me and I immediately said yes, but that I was only there to threaten everybody.

The two men laughed at this and I laughed too.

I was hoping to make friends with them so they'd let me go. I know how stupid that sounds but these were professionals and they didn't give a shit.

The stairs man said they weren't going to kill me.

'Thanks,' I said, and meant it.

He was all business and told me I was going to be shot in the legs, but they were afraid of ricochets so would I go out the back and lie on the grass?

I couldn't believe it.

Mitchell said something in the kitchen about not wanting them to do it there.

He was fat and baldy. The woman looked petrified.

The stairs man got annoyed and said, 'What do you want us to fucking do? We can't drive around like this.'

'What do I tell the guards?' said Mitchell.

The stairs man told him I couldn't go to the guards. They'd dump me miles away.

They argued about the noise gunshots would make.

The one in front of me suggested they use a sledgehammer on my legs.

They seemed to agree.

Mitchell was told to clear out for a few hours and take his missus with him.

And I was making up something you couldn't call a plan.

I didn't want to be a cripple for the rest of my life. I knew I'd have to pull the pistol from my pants and start shooting.

This was all pure panic.

The stairs man told Mitchell to go out the back way. But Mitchell said his keys were in the living-room.

As he walked down the hall to the door beside me I grabbed the Webley and fired it straight ahead. I didn't bother taking aim. The shot hit the man in front of me in the hip and he collapsed on top of me, knocking the pistol on to the floor.

Then the stairs man started shooting.

He hit the living-room door jamb and the wall before getting Mitchell in the back. And then there was a clicking sound.

His rifle had jammed.

An empty cartridge was stuck in the breach and he was trying to release it by working the bolt back and forth.

I was on my knees and I pulled the shotgun from the hall table.

I saw the empty cartridge fly out of his gun and he accidentally fired a shot into the bannister.

I pointed the shotgun up the stairs, and without being sure I had cocked or even fired, it discharged a deafening shot.

The man jerked backwards up the stairs and landed sitting at the bathroom door.

I knew he was dead.

I hit the man in the hall over the head with the gun 'til he lay still, then I rolled him over and took my pistol.

Mitchell was still alive. He was shaking and losing a lot of blood.

His wife was trying to unlock the back door and keep her child in front of her.

I dragged her back and the child hung on.

I got them on to the floor and told them to shut up.

I slapped the woman on the neck. I meant to hit her face but I was shaking.

She quietened down and I told her I wasn't going to hurt them.

Then my legs went from under me.

My knees just buckled and I was on the floor beside them.

There was a phone on the worktop and I was trying to remember Joe Murray's number. When I got through, he wasn't in the bar. It took ages for them to get him.

He couldn't believe what had happened.

He told me to keep the woman and the kid there and not to do anything.

He was sending someone over.

The woman wasn't moving. She just held her kid, who seemed to be asleep.

I went through to the hall.

Mitchell was still breathing but it was a funny sound.

His face was pressed against the hinge of the half-opened door.

I thought there was blood coming out of his mouth.

Upstairs the dead man was still holding his rifle. He was sitting in a shower of pellet wounds.

Most of them were in his chest and shoulder but a few were in his neck and one or two in his face.

I took the magazine from his gun.

It was only a matter of time before the noise brought the guards to the house.

I decided to keep my options open.

The first sign of trouble I was getting out as fast as I could.

I took Mitchell's keys from the living-room and went into the kitchen.

I asked Mrs. Mitchell if she was alright.

She just nodded and didn't look at me.

The kid looked drugged.

The kitchen had every modern appliance and for some reason that made me sad.

I was impatient. I wanted to get out.

I was watching Mitchell. He was breathing in shallow gasps.

The other man in the hall began to move a little bit. I told him to stay where he was. 'What are you going to do?' he asked me. I told him some friends of mine were coming and he could explain his side of it to the guards while I was miles away having a pint.

Then he said it. 'They're going to kill you.'

Now whether he meant his buddies or mine, I didn't know. But I began to worry.

How the fuck did these guys know I'd be coming that morning? Vinnie Rourke didn't like me and Joe Murray would more than likely send him.

And I'd made a pig's mickey of this.

Mrs. Mitchell could identify me and sooner or later they'd trace me back to Murray. Mrs. Mitchell was in trouble and I was in trouble. One of us would have to go.

I was watching the street. Across the road a woman was standing in her porch.

She'd heard something, but she didn't seem to know what to do. She went back inside and a car pulled up. The driver kept it running. Vinnie Rourke and two others got out. One of them looked into my car and nodded at Rourke. He adjusted something in his jacket and walked towards the house.

I just knew.

I ran into the kitchen and shouted at Mrs. Mitchell to tell me where their car was.

It was in a garage out the back.

I heard the doorbell.

I ran down the garden and smashed the garage door open.

Mitchell's car was huge, a Rover, and the lane at the back of the house was narrow.

I heard shouting from the house and I thought about just legging it through the gardens. I stood in the garage and I couldn't decide what to do.

Then someone came out the back and called my name. It was Chris Breen, an old buddy of Vinnie Rourke's. He saw me.

He was holding a small pistol.

'Where are you going?' he said, 'Come back.'

I didn't move.

'We've got to get out of here,' he said.

I stepped into the garden.

'What'll we do with the woman and the kid?' I asked him.

'Just come back in,' he said.

I kept my hand on the butt of my revolver and pointed it at him through my jacket.

And we went back into the house.

Rourke's other mate, who I didn't know, had gagged Mrs. Mitchell and he was tying her hands behind her back.

The little girl was trying to cling to her mother. The man looked up from what he was doing and nodded at me.

Rourke was in the hall, strangling the man I'd wounded.

When he finished he stood up and looked at me. 'This is a fucking mess,' he said, 'And I like the witnesses.' He nodded at Mrs. Mitchell. Chris Breen was pointing his gun at me.

'What are you doing?' I said.

He smiled and shrugged at me.

I shot him through my pocket and ran backwards, slamming the kitchen door on Rourke.

The one I didn't know put his hands up.

Chris Breen was sitting on the floor.

I'd got him in the mouth. He was looking around like this was the first stuff he'd ever seen. I heard the front door as Rourke ran out to the car.

'Lean over the sink,' I told Rourke's friend, 'Put your head in the sink. If you move, I'll kill you,' I told him.

I picked Mrs. Mitchell up and pushed her out the back. The kid clung to her leg.

I got them down to the garage and into the back of the car. Mrs. Mitchell lay across the back seat and the kid tumbled on to the floor.

The car was an automatic.

I had to keep my head to manoeuvre it into the lane.

I nudged it little by little and the lane opened up on to a road that ran around a green and then out to what looked like a main road.

I began to feel relieved, even jokey.

I asked Mrs. Mitchell if she wanted the radio on, and it seemed so ridiculous I started laughing. I was laughing and driving and I didn't know where I was going.

All I could think about was getting back to Greta and taking her away from Joe Murray. We could start again.

Then I heard sirens and knew we had to get out of the city.

We drove along Sundrive Road and Dolphin Road. Long roads with houses, garages, shops, undertakers, estate agents.

Eventually we hit the N4.

The sun was glinting in the rearview mirror. The eleven o'clock news had nothing yet. By lunchtime it'd be all over the place.

I pulled into a lay-by and shut the engine off. I leaned back and rubbed my face.

My hangover was coming back. I had hot flushes and shivers.

I got out and listened to the rain soaking into the ground, the odd car going past.

I bent over and got sick. The smell of whiskey and sugar made me retch again.

I knew I had to talk to Mrs. Mitchell, get her on my side. Buy us some time.

When I got myself together, I went back to the car. Mrs. Mitchell's head was against the door and the kid had climbed up on the seat beside her. She had a little blue dress on and one of her shoes was off.

Her hair was the same colour as her mother's but her face was chubbier.

Mrs. Mitchell was very thin.

Her hands looked sore from the clothes-line that tied them.

Her tracksuit bottoms were half off and I could have seen anything I wanted, but it just made me feel sick.

The kid was looking at me and Mrs. Mitchell was gasping for air.

There was snot all over her face and the rag around her mouth was soaking.

'Now Mrs. Mitchell,' I said, 'I'm going to talk to you and when you hear what I have to say, I'm going to untie you, do you understand me?' She nodded.

'When I untie you there's nowhere to run and I don't think you will if you listen to what I'm going to tell you. Can I trust you about these things?' She nodded again.

I sat in the driver's seat and began.

'Now listen, very soon the guards will be looking everywhere for us. There'll be roadblocks. I can't give you up because you can identify me. The men who came to your house were going to kill me and they were going to kill you.

They'll have gotten out of there without leaving a whole lot of clues. They're old time convicted rogues and they know what they're doing.

I'm in no position to go to the police and neither are you.

You knew what was going to happen to me and you didn't do anything.'

She shook her head and made a noise.

I told her I'd take her gag off in a minute and she could say what she liked then. I told her I'd only come to scare her husband and that everything else was his fault, except for the bunch of cunts I worked for.

'Now I have no intention of hurting you,' I told her. 'It was the men your husband hired who shot him. It was an accident.'

I made it clear I didn't want any of this but if we kept our heads and worked together we might live to tell the tale.

Joe Murray was sure to send Vinnie Rourke after us in case I blabbed to the guards as some sort of bargain.

He'd want Mrs. Mitchell too because she might link me to Murray.

Whoever the men who tried to break my legs were, if they were terrorists, their pals would be coming after us and of course, every guard in every shitty little fuckhole would have his eyes peeled.

She simply had to co-operate.

I asked her if she understood.

When she nodded, I leaned forward and took off the gag.

Then I pushed her up and undid her hands.

She sat up and held her kid.

'Thank you,' she said.

I didn't feel like talking anymore.

'We've got to change this car,' I said, 'Next town, we're changing this car.'

Then she said she didn't know what was going to happen at the house.

Mitchell's friends had come a few minutes before me. She didn't know who they were or what was going on.

I didn't say anything.

I just drove.

The news had been about a shooting and a possible kidnapping.

It was good being patchy. Right now the guards would be trying to figure out where Mrs. Mitchell might be without all the big search stuff.

She could be at the shops for all they knew.

Vinnie Rourke and the others must've gotten away. There were plenty of doctors Joe Murray knew who'd look after Chris Breen.

I reckoned Mr. Mitchell was dead.

I didn't say anything about it.

Mrs. Mitchell had her daughter on her lap. Things were peaceful.

I was beginning to see how lucky I'd been. Lucky or stupid.

I wondered which was worse, broken legs or being chased for killing someone.

Well I hadn't been caught, so maybe this was better.

I wanted to know what Greta would think.

This had to put me back at the centre of her thoughts. I wanted to know if she was worried about me. Did she think I was a fucking idiot?

Then I thought about Joe Murray putting it up her arse.

I called her a fucking bitch and apologised to Mrs. Mitchell.
I hadn't meant her. I hadn't meant her at all.

We drove into Kinnegad and I parked behind Jack's Bar, cum restaurant-B&B.

I asked Mrs. Mitchell if she wanted to get cleaned up.

She said okay. Then she asked me how I was for money.

I had about forty quid which wasn't going to get us very far.

She told me to take a map out of the glove compartment. There was a banklink card in the map. The name on it was Patrick Mitchell. 'Do you know the number?' I stupidly asked her.

She just took it.

We left the car there.

This was her chance. If she wanted one.

All she had to do was grab someone or make a run for it. I didn't know if she had enough reasons to trust me. Or if she was afraid of me.

But we found a vending machine and she withdrew two hundred quid.

For someone who'd just seen her husband shot she was remarkably calm.

'Maybe it's shock,' I thought.

She picked the girl up in her lean arms and we went into Harry's, another bar down the street.

I told them to go and get cleaned up and not be too long about it.

It was twenty to one and some lunch people were sitting about. The more the better as far as I was concerned. I sank a pint and got another one. I knew I had to slow down. I didn't need the attention. I sat at the window and pretended to read a paper someone had left there.

A Bus Eireann bus had stopped across the street. The driver was helping a woman get her luggage from the side.

I ordered sandwiches and tea and soup.

Then I thought about the girl and got chips and ice cream. I drank a small one and it calmed me down. Took the edge off.

Mrs. Mitchell seemed hungry which I also thought was really odd.

The kid ate the ice cream then the chips.

Mrs. Mitchell was dipping her sandwiches in her soup. I got her a brandy and she drank it.

She called the kid Monkey. 'Taste this, Monkey, wipe your hands.' The kid was very quiet and well behaved. Mrs. Mitchell asked where we should go.

I had a friend who lived in Sligo, Jeff.

He owned an estate agents.

I thought he could give us somewhere to put our heads down for a few days, watch the news. See which way the guards jumped. How much they knew about her husband or if they linked the whole thing to Murray.

She didn't say whether she thought it was a good idea or not. Which was good enough for me. I told them to wait.

And I went out to look for an old style Fiesta. These were cars I could start with very little hassle.

There was one outside the post office but there were too many people. I went the other way to where the road turns left at the end of the town.

There was a car park in front of some offices and a big factory.

I saw a woman get out of a 1981 Fiesta.

This was no bother.

I took out my keys and pretended to be wiping the windscreen of a Suzuki van.

When she was gone I went over and wrapped a stone in my jacket. I smashed the rear fly window on the driver's side.

When I reached in the fucking thing was open already. That's the country.

I kicked the cover off the steering column and pulled the wires out of the ignition lock. I got it going in a couple of seconds and drove around in front of Harry's.

Mrs. Mitchell didn't make a fuss. She just came out and got in.

I was surprised. She got in the front.

I told them to be careful of the glass and then we U-turned and headed west again.

Mrs. Mitchell wanted to know what we'd do if we came across a roadblock.

We decided to pretend we were married.

'What's your name?' I asked the girl.

She didn't answer me.

'Niamh,' said Mrs. Mitchell.

'Hello Niamh,' I said.

'Hello,' said Niamh.

We caught the headlines at half one.

Three bodies had been found in the house but hadn't been identified.

Mrs. Mitchell just looked out the window.

The traffic was heavy coming through Mullingar.

The rain came down in sheets.

I was relaxing. There wouldn't be roadblocks this far out.

I felt safe when we went through Longford without any hassle.

I was thinking about my friend, Jeff who'd moved to Boyle a few years before any of this.

He sold houses and land in Sligo, Leitrim, Roscommon. We'd only seen each other once or twice since he'd moved.

I'd stayed with him in a house no-one was buying, on the Shannon.

Greta had come and we drank and went out in a boat, all that sort of stuff.

Jeff had a wife and four kids, but he was very laid back. I trusted him and I hoped he could sort us out.

He knew what I did for a living and one time I'd helped him out.

A local councillor called Burke had hinted that Jeff would have to pay what he called an 'an administration fee' of five grand for planning permission for two bungalows Jeff was building for some people in Dublin.

Jeff said this was bollocks and told the councillor to fuck off.

A couple of nights later while Jeff was having a piss in the pub, someone punched him on the back of the head.

He broke a front tooth on the tiling.

He got a few kicks and someone told him to get his responsibility as a citizen together. And all that tat.

This told him that Burke must have been behind it.

He phoned me in Dublin.

He was scared. He wanted Burke off his back but didn't want to know the details.

I drove to Boyle on a Tuesday afternoon.

Burke spent his afternoons in a pub called the Riverside. He drank with men who worked for him. Delivering peat briquettes.

They watched the telly for racing results.

Burke never spoke to anyone unless they spoke to him.

I watched him mill five or six pints and when I saw him get ready to go I slipped out in front of him.

I followed him home. He drove a Mercedes.

He lived across from his farm which was a series of fields along a bend in the river. It was a nice spot.

I sat and waited, enjoying the peace and quiet. I wanted to make sure he was alone. He had no children. His wife left the house around five. She was a nurse.

A few minutes later, Burke came out with wellies and a walking stick.

He went down to the river and looked at the bank. There was some flooding.

I got out and waved at him.

He turned and waved back.

I walked towards him with a friendly smile.

He gripped his stick a little tighter and watched me carefully. He was much bigger than me and I knew I'd have to fuck him up very quickly.

When I was about fifteen feet away from him, I started to say 'I wonder if you could tell me where I might find a place called . . . '

And I kicked the shit out of him.

I kicked him as he tried to run away.

I kicked him on the ground and I hit him with his stick until I was exhausted.

Then I picked him up and punched and dragged him back up to his house.

He collapsed on the driveway but I kicked his arse and got him inside.

'Where's the kitchen?' I asked him.

'I don't have any money here,' he said.

I told him to shut up.

I didn't want to tell him Jeff had sent me in case Burke's friends did something to him.

I wanted to fuck him up generally so that he'd be too scared to do anything to anybody. And I wanted him in the kitchen because that's where people keep their knives.

Mrs. Mitchell wanted to use the toilet so we stopped in Carrick on Shannon.

The news had that one of the dead men had been identified as Dublin businessman, Patrick Mitchell.

The Gardai were interviewing witnesses at the scene.

A woman had seen three men come out of the house and one of them was hurt. I knew that was Chris Breen.

Two of the men had gone in Vinnie Rourke's car and another had taken mine.

They were afraid of my car being linked to Joe Murray. This wasn't working out so bad. There were no definite leads.

When Mrs. Mitchell and Niamh came back I said, 'Listen, if there's anyone you want to call and say you're okay, I think you should, but just don't tell them where you are yet.'

She just nodded.

I asked her if she was alright.

I was curious at how calm she was.

'Are you in shock?' I said.

She asked me what I meant.

I said I didn't know and she laughed.

I was beginning to think Mrs. Mitchell was a bit of a loolah.

We drove over a bridge and a sign said Boyle, 12 miles.

'My friend, Jeff,' I was telling her, 'always has empty houses, secluded, we can probably stay somewhere like that for a day or two and work things out. Is that okay?'

'Yes,' she said. As if she was annoyed at me. Then Niamh said something about a tree and we smiled.

I was watching the road and thinking about what people were like.

I was tired. There was a house right beside the road. I wanted to live there so I could pull in, sit by the fire and have a few drinks. Eat my dinner and go to bed and in bed, my pretty wife would tell me she wasn't my judge and I'd sleep and sleep and dream until the next thing I'd do which would be an interesting thing.

And no-one would bother me.

The day was dark and the rain becoming torrential when we got to Boyle.

Mrs. Mitchell waited in the car.

I went over to Jeff's offices beside the memorial and I saw him through the door.

He was talking to a woman who was typing at a computer.

I looked around and went in.

'Jesus,' said Jeff.

I smiled and asked him if he had a minute.

'Come on,' he said, and we went into his office.

'I'm in trouble,' I told him.

'I'm going to be straight with you. I've killed someone and I need somewhere to go.' 'Is this the thing on the radio?' he said.

'It's not my fault,' I told him.

'They're looking for a woman and a kid.'

He was smarter than he looked.

'It's not a kidnap,' I told him, 'They're in the car.' I told him what had happened.

He sat down and didn't look well for a few minutes and then he said, 'Come on.'

I followed him out. He asked his secretary for some keys.

'Wait 'til you see this place,' he said.

We went out into the rain.

'Get them,' said Jeff, 'We'll take my car and dump that one later.'

And as I ran across to the Fiesta, he shouted, 'It's nice to see you.' I swung around and we were laughing.

I told Mrs. Mitchell we'd been sorted out.

Niamh had been sick.

'That's okay, Niamh,' I said, 'It's not our car.'

Jeff pulled alongside and Mrs. Mitchell took Niamh into the back.

I introduced everyone.

Jeff said, 'How are you Niamh, chicken, a bit car sick?' 'She's alright now,' said Mrs. Mitchell.

'And how are you?' said Jeff.

'I'm okay,' she said.

Then Jeff said, 'It's over now, I promise you'll all be safe.'

Mrs. Mitchell said this was the worst rain she'd ever seen, and Jeff asked us if it was raining in Dublin.

I wondered if I was in a car full of fucking loopers.

We drove for about ten miles with the wipers on full tilt.

Jeff was telling us a story about a time his car was stuck in the mud after he'd been drinking at some festival in Galway.

It was one of those stories where everyone ends up covered in mud, pushing the wrong car into a lake.

I closed my eyes and listened to Jeff.

And I could feel Niamh's breath in my ear as she stood between the seats.

I wondered if things were getting better or if Jeff was just one of those people.

'And here we are,' he said.

We turned through a pair of huge gates and drove up a tree-lined avenue.

And in a wide hollow was a house as big as the GPO.

'Be it ever so humble,' said Jeff.

'Look where we're going to stay, Niamh,' said Mrs. Mitchell.

Jeff was grinning to save his life.

We went in through high narrow doors.

We were in a tiled hallway.

The door straight ahead lead to a similar back hall and we could see a huge garden which sloped down to the Shannon where it was wide and islands stretched across to a newly planted forest.

We walked around looking for ghosts.

Jeff was talking to us.

But I wasn't listening. I was too busy smelling the air.

The rooms were empty and recently refloored.

The boards gave off an unexpected warmth.

The rain hammered off the windows.

I stood in the darkening ballroom.

Jeff took Mrs. Mitchell with Niamh in her arms up to the next floor.

I heard him tell her how surprisingly cheap a place like this was.

I sat with my back to the wall and put my revolver on my lap.

I closed my eyes and listened to the rain and the wind.

I was dreaming about the heart of the countryside beating.

I was in the veins like a sickness and Greta's hands were in my clean hair and we lay just beneath the clouds wondering when the storm would end.

I woke to sunshine blazing across the floor. I was wrapped in a quilt and soft little hands were on my face. Niamh ran across to the windows in her bare feet.

I heard voices. Laughing. Children shouting. My revolver was pressing against my shoulderblade.

I sat up. It was eleven o'clock.

Jeff came in and said, 'You're alive.' Fucking comedian.

He had a flask.

He sat down beside me and I drank a cup of coffee.

He told me he had brought his wife, Marie, and the kids over. Marie and Mrs. Mitchell were organising a picnic. This was blowing my mind.

I wanted to know if we were safe.

'I think so,' he said.

He showed me the papers.

People seemed to think it was some sort of fucked up IRA thing, which suited me fine.

The Guards were appealing for information about the cars.

They didn't have any registrations.

They found Mitchell's car in Kinnegad, and they were looking for the Fiesta.

Nobody had seen us yet.

Jeff had it stashed in the garage of a house he was selling which didn't get many viewers.

As long as nothing linked it to me or Murray no-one would find us up here in Leitrim, which is where we turned out to be.

Jeff gave me clean clothes and razors and stuff. I showered upstairs in an en-suite bathroom.

Out the window I could see Mrs. Mitchell and Marie organising blankets on the lawn.

Everything was on a huge plastic sheet.

Jeff was playing with the kids.

He picked Niamh up and swung her around, chasing the others with her in his arms.

She was in hysterics.

On the blankets Jeff's baby was lying on her belly, rolling onto her back.

I went down.

Marie kissed me and gave me a long hug.

Mrs. Mitchell smiled at me.

I sat down and played with the baby.

She squeezed my fingers tightly, even though she was tiny.

I liked the pressure.

There were sandwiches, meat, salad, cake, wine, beer and coffee all on paper plates spread over the blankets.

I smoked one of Marie's Marlboro's and had a beer.

I held the baby on my lap and we all laughed at her.

Mrs. Mitchell sat beside me and drank Piât D'Or from a paper cup.

She said she hadn't seen Niamh have so much fun in ages.

'They're great kids,' I said.

Marie took the baby from me to change her nappy. Jeff was rounding up the children.

I asked Mrs. Mitchell if she'd seen the papers. She said she had and then became upset. I tried to comfort her, but she pulled away from me and said 'Look, you're not my friend, okay?'

I nodded.

We didn't say anything for a minute.

Then she said, 'Sorry.'

And I said, 'No.'

She said she'd made a call.

'To who?' I asked her.

But Marie came back, shouting 'Come on, everybody.'

The kids stuffed themselves.

I was starving too.

I must've ate about a loaf of seafood sandwiches which were Marie's thing.

I drank a few beers, but I really wanted to get Mrs. Mitchell on her own and ask her who the fuck she'd called.

So I asked her to come for a walk.

We went down to the river.

The baby was crying.

'Who did you ring?' I asked her.

She sat on a rock and put her feet in the water.

'Oh that's freezing,' she said, 'I thought it'd be warmer.'

I smacked the back of her head and grabbed her hair.

I told her that if she fucked me around, I'd break every bone in her body.

I'd really lost my temper.

She didn't shout. She didn't make a sound.

I let her go and she said, 'I rang Niamh's father, alright?'

I wanted to know what she was talking about.

'Patrick Mitchell wasn't her father,' she said, 'I had been seeing someone.'

She gave me a story about some teenage sweetheart coming back into her life a year or two after she'd married Mitchell.

She wouldn't sleep with Mitchell and he was going bananas. He was going to move them all to England which is why he was trying to sort the Joe Murray thing out.

But there was no way she was going.

She wanted to be with this man.

But he was a journalist who travelled around a lot and he wasn't ready to settle down and support them.

That's why she was still with Mitchell when he died.

Like so many fucking things.

She needed a roof over her head.

So she'd rung this man in Paris saying what had happened, but that she was safe.

She hadn't told him where she was but he was coming to Ireland.

'You have to believe me,' she said.

I did believe her.

For one thing, it seemed to explain her less than widowly grief.

'You make me sick,' I said. And walked off. She chased me and punched my back.

'What do you mean?' she shouted.

But I knew I hadn't meant her.

I was sorry I'd said it.

She became upset again and this time when I put my arm around her, she cried into my chest.

And I was thinking about Joe Murray on top of Greta.

I told her I was sure it would work out.

'Come on Mrs. Mitchell,' I said, 'Let's have a drink.'

She laughed at me calling her Mrs. Mitchell and said her name was Anna.

I told her I was sorry for all the shit that had happened. But I was trying to feel sorry and I don't think I really did.

Not that I was glad. I don't mean that at all.

She seemed to cheer up a little bit then and we spent the rest of the afternoon drinking and watching the children.

The baby fell asleep in my arms.

Jeff went down and swam. The kids jumped around on the shore and he splashed them.

The rest of us smoked and chatted occasionally.

At dusk it began to get a bit chilly.

We went inside and sat in the ballroom.

The children were tired and it was time for Jeff to bring his family home.

Marie was saying goodbye to Mrs. Mitchell.

I wondered if I should ring Joe Murray.

But Jeff said he'd be back in the morning and we could decide what to do then.

Mrs. Mitchell had slept upstairs the night before but she moved her stuff down beside mine.

When Jeff was gone she laid Niamh down in the quilt and we spoke quietly for a while.

Her boyfriend was a freelance writer and she seemed to love him very much. He knew he was Niamh's father, but he'd only seen her three times.

Mr. Mitchell had thought Niamh was his.

She had been conceived during a two-week daily sex session at the Mitchell's house while he was at work.

I felt sorry for the poor bastard.

Mrs. Mitchell hoped to get out of the country without being involved in any investigation.

We joked for a while about what colour she should dye her hair to avoid being recognised. She wanted to know what I was going to do. I didn't know. I told her I hadn't any commitments or ties.

I sort of wanted to talk about Greta but I didn't know where to begin.

We settled down for the night.

I could feel them lying beside me and when I listened to them breathing it felt like my soul was being bleached.

I woke to the sound of glass breaking.

'What is it?' I heard Mrs. Mitchell say.

It was pitch dark.

I took my pistol and told her to stay where she was.

I made my way to the front door.

It was open and the breeze filled the hall.

I couldn't see anyone.

I moved my way back toward the ballroom, feeling for a light switch.

'Mrs. Mitchell?' I whispered.

A torch went on and something bounced off my head.

I was very groggy.

I could see that dawn was coming and that there were people in the room.

My hands were cuffed behind me and I had no clothes on.

I was sitting on the floor.

I passed out again.

Then I was slapped.

This time it was brighter.

Vinnie Rourke's friend, Seamus Parker was slapping me.

'Get you're fucking hands off me,' I said.

Someone kicked me in the back. I collapsed and I couldn't move.

The feeling came back gradually and I wished it wouldn't.

'Get him up,' someone said.

I was dragged to my feet by Seamus Parker and someone else I didn't know.

Vinnie Rourke stood in front of me and quick as he could, he gave me three digs, two in the stomach and one in the face.

He did it so fast I knew he was showing off.

I took a step backwards but they held me steady.

'Where's Joe Murray?' I asked.

They all started digging me.

I was surprised how weak their punches were.

Maybe it was they were up all night.

I was getting worried about Mrs. Mitchell and Niamh. But I didn't want to say anything.

I didn't want to draw attention to them.

I wanted them to be forgotten.

Vinnie Rourke grabbed my bollocks and gave them a good wrench.

It was agony, but it was sort of funny.

I asked him if he was enjoying himself.

He got a bit annoyed.

I said I never knew he was a poof.

That did the job. He let go and told me he'd show me who was a poof.

He kicked my legs so hard I was leaping in Seamus Parker's arms.

Then I was on the floor.

I knew he'd break my neck if he kept kicking me. I was passing out.

I saw Greta and Mrs. Mitchell leading me up some stairs in newly painted flats beside a river. There was a war and they were looking after me.

Then I was drenched on the floor.

Vinnie Rourke had poured a bucket of water over me.

My left eye was closing.

I could just see Joe Murray sitting on a chair above me.

Nobody said anything.

I smiled at him and he looked away.

Then he asked me what I thought I was playing at.

I tried to speak and something fell out of my mouth.

I ran my tongue along the gaps in my teeth.

'For fuck's sake,' said Murray.

I managed to say 'How . . . ?'

'How did we find you?' he said, 'Don't be dense. Greta knew where you'd go. You see,' he said, 'She loves me so she told me. How does that make you feel?'

I was disappointed, but something cheered me up. And it was something I knew about and Joe Murray didn't. Greta didn't love anybody. He didn't know her at all.

'What are you grinning at?' he said. 'You little bastard. We looked after your friend. We looked after that fucker.'

I knew he must have found out where we were from Jeff. But Jeff wouldn't have told him simply because he was asked nicely.

'It was like the towering fucking inferno,' he said.

I thought he might be bluffing but I wasn't very hopeful that Jeff and his family were still alive.

I was waiting for him to get on with it and shoot me.

I wondered whose fault this was.

'And I suppose you want to know about flat chest Mitchell and the sprog,' said Murray and the way he said it told me everything.

When I was out cold, they'd had a party.

Maybe that dream I'd had of her when I was getting that kicking was her soul and she had met me while things were happening to her body. I still like to think that.

Murray was talking.

'Greta did us a favour telling me where you were, and we're going to do something for her. She asked us to let you live.'

I couldn't believe it. She had been thinking about me. She wanted me to be alive.

He went on.

'We've worked something out. In a few hours you'll be arrested here. There'll be evidence the Mitchells were here, but not enough to completely fuck you. Keep your mouth shut, make something up and you'll get accessory, five to ten years we reckon.'

He got up and signalled the others to go.

Then he said, 'Mention me or anybody and we'll kill you. I'm only doing this for Greta. She says I can trust you. And I have to trust her. Don't I? I mean, I'm not young any more. I have to make a commitment.'

I motioned to him with my head and he leaned over me.

'Just don't put it in her arse,' I said.

I don't know if he heard me or not.

He just got up and left.

I lay there throbbing from the kicks and I thought my heart would burst.

Sure enough towards afternoon the guards came.

I was taken to hospital and I wouldn't answer any questions.

I turned off in every interrogation.

I just thought about Greta.

I was wondering what she was doing at the precise moment I was thinking about her.

Funny, I always imagined her having a bath.

Eventually I confessed to a kidnapping.

But I said I was only the driver.

I didn't know that Mitchell had been killed and I was waiting for a ransom for us to release Mrs. Mitchell.

The other kidnappers had double-crossed me and beat me. I didn't know their real names. I thought they were English.

The Guards saw this for the rubbish it was, but it was all they had.

They'd found me tied up and in bits. They knew I couldn't have done that to myself, and although they linked me to Jeff, whoever had done the arson job on his house had made it look accidental enough.

My army record was good, I'd never been arrested before.

Mrs. Mitchell and Niamh were never found.

No bodies, no murder-charge.

At my trial I think everyone thought I was some sort of idiot.

But fuck that. I got ten years.

I didn't think very much for the next few weeks.

I just went along day by day.

I felt sad all of the time.

But I'm not sure what I felt sad about.

And I know how stupid that sounds.

Then the sad feeling went and I just thought about Greta.

I wanted to kill Joe Murray and Vinnie Rourke.

It was the only reason I wanted to get out.

And after that I didn't really feel anything.

Sometimes I woke up thinking Niamh's hands were on my face and I would wish that everyone was still alive. But these were more feelings than thoughts.

They ran through me and they were spilt milk.

I knew nothing good could come out of what had happened because of everybody's stupidity.

Then one day someone was put in my cell with me.

His name was Tom Vander.

He was twenty, a burglar.

We didn't speak much to begin with, which isn't to say we weren't friendly.

He didn't make many friends and pretty much stayed on his own.

Then one evening we just sort of got talking.

He had started breaking into houses around where he lived, in Clontarf, about a year before.

He liked the feeling of being in someone else's house with all their private things.

Sometimes, he'd even take a bath.

I thought this was very funny.

He never stole much. Just cash, if he found it, but he never looked very hard.

The odd time he'd watch their videos or look through their books.

He might sound a bit spacey, but he was alright. He was a good laugh.

We never bothered each other if one of us wasn't in a talky mood.

We were happy enough reading or just listening to tapes.

One night I told him all about Mrs. Mitchell and Niamh and everything that had happened.

He didn't say anything about it and I was glad he didn't. He just knew it was something you couldn't say anything about.

I told him about Greta and he told me about his girlfriends and how he'd had sex up a tree one time.

That night I heard him wanking in the bunk above me and I wanked too.

We wanked a lot after that. We knew when either of us were doing it and we made up filthy stories while we did it.

This usually ended in hysterics.

Then one blazing summer's day, Tom was released.

I knew he was getting out but I hadn't thought about it much. He was delighted and I was too. But then I felt crap because one day he was there and the next he wasn't and I couldn't talk to him any more.

He went to England.

He wrote for a while and then he got engaged and didn't write after that.

My own company wasn't good enough for me anymore.

And it wasn't that I wanted to be entertained or anything, I wanted to make someone else happy.

I wanted to be there when they needed me.

I don't live in Ireland any more.

I drink too much and I hardly go out.

I sometimes wonder about the type of person I am, but not for long.

I'm no good.

Sometimes when the clouds are low and I look out the window with one eye on the pillow I still think about Mrs. Mitchell and Niamh and Jeff's family.

And I think about Greta and the time I saw her last year.

It was a filthy wet day and she got out of a big car with a man twice her age.

I thought about walking up to her but I was trying to get out of the rain.

THIS LIME TREE BOWER

For Jack McPherson and Gina

A delight
Comes sudden on my heart, and I am glad
As I myself were there! Nor in this bower,
This little lime tree bower, have I not marked
Much that has soothed me.

... No sound is dissonant which tells of life.

Samuel Taylor Coleridge,
'This Lime Tree Bower My Prison',
1797

This Lime Tree Bower was first performed at the Crypt Arts Centre, Dublin, on 26 September 1995, an Íomhá Ildánach/Fly by Night co-production. The cast were:

JOE	Ian Cregg
RAY	Conor Mullen
FRANK	Niall Shanahan

Lighting by Paul Winters
Designed by John O'Brien and Conor McPherson
Produced by Philip Gray
Directed by Conor McPherson

The play was subsequently performed with the same cast at the Bush Theatre, London, from 3rd July 1996.

Lighting by Paul Russell
Directed by Conor McPherson

Characters
JOE, *seventeen*
RAY, *early thirties*
FRANK, *twenties*

All remain on stage throughout, and are certainly aware of each other.

JOE

Damien came to our school halfway through the term.

He was different from everybody else there.

Even his uniform made him look good.

He had a long fringe, bleached, and he had a tan.

He always smoked and he never went home at lunchtime. I found out that he didn't live too far away, and he probably had the coolest bike in the whole school, but at lunchtime, he hung around.

I started smoking too, so I could talk to him at little break behind the religion room. It was completely fucking disgusting.

You were supposed to be dying for a pull and about nine blokes would be sharing a fag. By the time it came around to you it was just a soaking wet filter.

And you had to drag on it like you'd die without it.

But I got to talk to Damien.

I pretended my bike was broken and I brought sandwiches in so I could hang around at big break.

The lads who stayed in all got chips in the Chinese, which I wouldn't get because of what my dad had told me about them.

The lads who ate them all had huge spots, except for Damien.

He was only in three of my classes, and one of them was Civics, which we only had once a week, but I could never wait for him to come in.

He was never on time and in the mornings if I was in a room where I could see the driveway, I'd watch for him.

I never once saw him arrive but he'd always be there.

That's the way it is when you like someone – you can never see them.

I tried to tell Frank, my brother, about Damien, but he called me a poofter and told me to go asleep.

Frank was five years older than me and worked with my dad in our chipper.

I only worked there during the holidays.

It was never busy 'til then.

No-one comes to the seaside when it's raining, which is weird, because that's when I liked it best.

When it was all grey and the waves splashed up on the road is when I liked it.

Those sort of days my dad had a pint in Reynolds' and read the paper.

I used to go in and sit with him sometimes.

Like on a Saturday.

He told me once that drinking is no way for a man to sort anything out, but that he only found out too late.

I told him not to be silly.

Frank said that Dad's problems were none of his doing.

He owed a big loan to Simple Simon McCurdie.

Simple Simon was a councillor and owned the bookies down the street.

Frank said he was far from simple.

We didn't know how he got the name.

But he had it.

And that's what we called him.

I'm quite shrewd and I know how to do things in ways that don't look really obvious.

That's how I made friends with Damien.

We'd just find ourselves standing together.

I saw what bands he had, written on his bag and on his journal.

I let on to like them too.

And because he'd come halfway through the term, he didn't know anyone.

Sometimes I'd pretend not to see him and he'd still come over to me.

So I knew he liked me.

He was kicked out of his last school for being on the mitch and smoking in P.E.

He had told a teacher to fuck off and she had just got out of hospital or something and she started crying.

He was lucky to get into our school because not many places would take someone like that.

But then, my school was a dump.

Someone who lived near Damien said he hadn't been expelled at all.

He had left because he was always being slagged for only having one ball.

But somebody always says something.

I reckon our school had pity on him because he needed somewhere to do his leaving.

He told me about the girls he'd shagged and how he could always tell when someone was a virgin.

I blushed so badly that I had to pretend to blow my nose so he wouldn't see.

He asked me to bonk off school one Friday.

I'd never done it before and I knew I'd be killed.

But Damien said he was an expert forger and he'd give me a brilliant note.

We arranged to meet at the roundabout on the dual carriageway at nine o' clock.

I was waiting for ages.

I thought everyone was looking at me.

And I knew that Miss Brosnan, our biology teacher, used to drive around looking for boys on the mitch when she had a free class. She had huge tits and we used to pretend there was something wrong with the microscopes so she'd bend over to have a look.

I was imagining her catching me on the mitch and making me fuck her as a punishment.

I was too scared to go off on my own and I was going to go in late and get detention.

But then Damien showed up.

He didn't even have his uniform on.

We cycled around the suburbs and stayed off the main roads. It felt brilliant.

All the people were at work.

I saw women wheeling kids out of the supermarket and I thought about me being with my mum when I was like that.

We went into the park.

It was dark under the trees and we scrambled up and down the hills.

Then it was nearly one and we sat down and ate our lunch.

We could see two girls from Holy Faith going through the park to the shops.

Damien knew them.

They were gorgeous and I felt like an ugly bollox.

One was blonde and one was dark like she was foreign.

Damien made them laugh about people they knew and I didn't.

I wanted to hold their hands and stroll through town with lots of money.

They didn't say anything to me, but they looked at me like if I was with Damien, there must be something good about me.

But they couldn't see what.

I sucked in my cheeks and pretended not to be interested.

I fiddled with my gears and broke them.

When the girls were gone we sat under the trees where we could see the beach.

My stomach was all tingly.

Damien said the blonde one, Tara, would ride anybody. She had had it off with most of his friends and Damien had screwed her when he was fourteen.

I asked him how it had happened and I immediately felt like a cretin.

Damien just said, 'Got a boner. Stuck it in.'

Then he went off for a piss and he was gone for ages.

I had to go looking for him, but when I found him I let on I was just cycling around.

He told me his dad was living with some woman and that his mum had had him when she was sixteen.

He started saying how cool she was and we should go home and see her.

I told him school wasn't over yet.

He said his mum couldn't give two shits.

They lived out by the Old Strand Road where all the Protestants lived.

The house had a long front garden with high trees. There was a boat in the drive but Damien said it didn't go.

There was a lawnmower in the hall and the carpet was filthy.

There was a spicy smell.

We had toast and peanut butter and watched MTV. There were bottles everywhere.

I looked out the back. The garden was lower than the front.

Then Damien's mum came in.

She was small and she had jeans and runners.

She didn't look like any of the mums I knew.

She had too much make-up and I could see she had no bra.

She ignored me and asked Damien why he wasn't in school.

A man came in behind her and went straight out the back.

A huge dog ran after him and the man took off his shirt.

I watched him run around with the dog and then he jumped into a muddy pond at the bottom of the garden, with his pants still on.

Damien shouted at his mum not to give him a hard time – she was doing his head in.

She stopped giving out then and gave him a kiss.

He put his hand on her arse and she was looking at me and giggling.

I was sort of laughing too, but I didn't think it was funny.

I was being false.

I went out pretending I really had a thing for dogs. The dog didn't come near me though. I sat in the kitchen door and watched the man.

He was putting his head under the water and coming up saying, 'Jeeesus, Jeeesus Christ!'

Damien came out and I asked him who the man was. But Damien didn't know. He must've been a friend of his mum's he thought.

The man shouted at us not mind him because he was a bit pissed.

Damien's mum came out and said, 'Peter, What are you doing?'

Then she laughed and ran down to the pond.

I went home then.

Damien wanted me to stay but I felt funny.

Then I was too early.

I had to wait outside Simple Simon's bookies for a quarter of an hour 'til school was over.

Simple Simon saw me and came out.

He was really fat and he scared the shit out of me.

He leaned against the door-frame all chummy with his arms folded.

He didn't say anything for a minute, like we were really used to each other.

Then he asked how Dad was.

I said alright, thanks.

'Good, good,' he said.

He was always saying that, 'Good, good,' like it was some catchphrase the audience loved.

Then he showed what a bollox he was and asked me if I was on the mitch.

I said no.

And he said, 'Why are you hanging around here then? What are you waiting for?'

He said it like he was going to slap me but then he broke his shit laughing.

I gave him the false laugh I was getting good at and cycled off.

He told me to say hello to Frank for him.

Frank said Simple Simon was a fucking leech when I told him.

He was wiping tables and filling ketchup in our sit-down part.

Dad was out the back with his head under the bonnet. He asked me how school was.

I shouted fine and ran upstairs.

I lay in my room and wanked and thought about the girls in the park, and they loved me because there had been a nuclear blast and there was no-one left in the world.

Only us. They had to share me.

They had to take turns.

It was just to have a good wank.

Because the girl I really fancied was Deborah Something.

She lived down the road and I'd only ever seen her from the side.

My sister Carmel was in the shower because her boyfriend Ray was coming.

He had a great car because he had this really good job lecturing in a college.

He gave out about it a lot.

He said the thickest people he ever met were all in third level institutions.

One time he showed us a journal called *Ethics* because he had an article in it.

I couldn't grasp what it was about but you could see he was clever.

Him and Dad and Frank would sit up drinking whiskey and watching the late news programmes. Then they'd give out about the politicians and the reporters and anybody they saw.

They slagged what everybody said and the way everybody looked.

That was the way it was.

I don't know what Ray was doing hanging around with my sister.

Maybe he wasn't clever all the time.

Or just blind.

RAY

I woke up on a cold October morning in bed with one of my students.

What was her name? I can't remember.

I got up, put on my Dunnes Stores' jumper and underpants.

I always wore khaki trousers in those days.

It was kind of . . . a thing with me.

The room was freezing.

All the usual shit. Paper light shade, Stone Roses poster, a load of fucking awful books I'd never read and all the empty bottles of wine she'd drunk over the last God knows.

Her hair was sticking out over the quilt.

She was a bit of a chubby yoke, and for a minute I felt like hopping back in and giving her one. From behind.

But it was a passing yen and I had a lecture to give at twelve.

I felt like absolute shite.

I was putting on weight and I needed a haircut and a shave.

Had to wash my face in cold water.

Didn't bother waking her up. Fuck her.

I went down and got into the Saab.

And just my luck, it was always a bitch to start on a cold morning.

By the time I got it going she was looking out the window.

I pretended not to see.

She turned away quickly and I just knew she was going to leg it down to the garden. But by that time I was long gone.

Going down the dual carriageway, me, Pat, Elaine and the fucking Morning Crew, and my hangover was coming into its own.

I'd started the afternoon before with a quiet pint in the student bar.

Now I always drank in the student bar because I hate academics.

I don't really like students either, but there you are.

Well a few of them joined me and they're buying me pints.

And what do you know? It's nine o'clock and there's a disco on.

Girl from my third year utilitarianism group in a leather mini and I'm up dancing.

One of the kids . . .

And I was thinking about these sort of German bohemians in Hamburg trying to understand the Beatles. Like these kids trying to work me out. See what makes me tick.

We paused for cocktails. There was a tequila promotion on. Few of them and I'm back up again.

For a minute, I forgot who I was.

And then I remembered and I spun round and round like a kid and it was all coming back and then I puked right there in front of everybody.

People slipped in it, the place was mayhem.

The lights came on and for some reason I offered to pay for the mess.

Then it was time for lifts home.

Out into the wind and drizzle.

There's five of them in the fucking car.

I was annoyed now.

Someone put on a tape. It was a comedy thing which wasn't remotely fucking funny.

First stop, Blackrock. Two girls get out.

They're talking philosophy in the back of the car. This fucking kid with long manky hair is nearly screaming some stupid theory about Karl Popper so I'll hear him and . . . remember him forever, or give him a job or something.

And everyone else is going, 'Just shut the fuck up, Vyvyan.' Back across the dueller into Goatstown.

Then it's just me and her.

She lives in Mount Merrion.

She invites me in.

I check she doesn't live with her parents – happened to me before when I was working as a tutor in England.

I was banging this first year in the morning and her mother came in to wake her for college. You can't take anything for granted.

It was cool. So in we go. I crash on her bed. I wake up. Three in the morning. I roll over. We do it.

It was shite.

Anyway, into college.

I parked behind the bar and thought about how long it had been since I was in there. Eleven and a half. Eleven and a fucking half hours.

I had to give a twelve o' clock in Theatre O. I'd enough time to get a cure.

I sat in the filthy bar and laid into about four gin and tonics because I'd heard somewhere that they were supposed to be good for a hangover.

But that's probably bullshit too.

Nothing works except getting pissed again.

It's a dreadful fucking world, isn't it?

I made up my mind not to feel guilty.

Carmel could never find out. Our lives were too separate.

Of course, this was something I could lose my job over. But it was just the state I was in I couldn't give a fuck.

I waffled my way through the lecture.

There were only about twenty there.

The rest probably all had hangovers.

I fucking turned up. Ingrates.

Up in my office the wind was howling.

I watched the trees blowing.

I went and had a huge shite.

Then I put my head on my desk and snoozed.

I dreamt I'd organised a recording of *Under Milk Wood* in my flat.

John Rawls came down from the mountains and his wife was choosy about what she ate.

I woke with someone knocking at the door. I looked at my watch.

Three o'clock. Twelve hours since I'd rolled over.

And there she was at the door.

She came in and started crying.

I gave her a tissue. Told her it wasn't a big deal.

I joked with her and she cheered up.

With some girls it's just about pushing the right buttons, isn't it?

We drove to a quiet pub out near Rathfarnham.

After a few drinks and something to eat, I said, 'Friends again?' She smiled.

Yeah, we'd been stupid. We admitted it.

But we were adults.

We could put it behind us.

There was nothing to worry about.

Inside, I was seething.

Thinking about what a stupid fat bitch she was. Doing this on me. Her little moment of glory.

I couldn't breathe. My stomach was full of acid.

I nearly lost my temper but I kept my cool.

At seven I gave her a lift into town.

She was going to the Stag's Head.

All I needed now was for her to have a bun in the oven. That'd be just fucking great.

It was time to see Carmel.

Carmel had these . . . country virtues.

That whole Greek idea of the good life.

The life lived well.

I fancied a few beers with her brother, Frank. Shoot the shit for a while and then later, when everyone was in bed me and Carmel would go up to her room.

You see, I was sort of in the middle of an experiment in those days.

I wanted to have a really vigorous fuck and break the condom.

Driving down the Malahide Road, I touched ninety twice.

Life in the old girl yet.

FRANK

I remember that Friday.

The weather had been rotten all week.

It was freezing when I woke up.

Dad was out the back, messing with the car. I told him to leave it and let Ray have a look. Ray knew a few bits and pieces about engines and that. He was a great driver. And he usually called over to see Carmel on a Friday.

Dad was always fucking around with the engine. It was an old Peugeot 205.

He never went anywhere in it since Mum died. He didn't have the will.

He didn't have any reason to go in it.

And this made him think there was something wrong with it.

People always blame something, don't they?

I normally got up about eleven.

We opened at twelve on the dot.

I had just sort of drifted into working with Dad. He couldn't afford to pay me a fortune.

But I was living at home.

I had no overheads.

It was boring but it was better than nothing.

Because there's nothing worse than a seaside town in the winter when there's nobody about.

We had our regulars at lunchtime.

They'd come around from the bank and the shopping centre.

That was a little belt for about an hour.

Then about four, people would send their kids in for the tea.

Friday teatime was always good.

Sevenish, it'd slack off 'til the pubs closed.

We stayed open 'til one at the weekends, half eleven, twelve on weekdays.

It was usually just me and Dad.

But sometimes Joe would drag his heels around, 'working'.

But he hated it.

Carmel was too busy to help.

She was being trained as something at the new financial services centre in the city, which sounded good. But she never said much about it, so it was probably a load of shite.

I had a couple of nights off, mid week, when Dad just did take-aways.

There was nothing to do, except sit in Reynolds' bar and listen to the old lads going on about when the INLA split from the officials and all that sort of thing they could get into a fight about.

If Simple Simon McCurdie was there, they'd use him as a sort of umpire.

He'd sit at the bar with a bottle of Blackbush and nod at them wisely whenever anyone mentioned Seamus Costello or Cathal Goulding.

I'd head back to give Dad a hand about eleven.

First thing in the morning, I'd turn on the fat and the telly.

Anne and Nick were my favourite, Nick always seemed to be taking the piss out of Anne. I'd have it on in the back and just be listening to it while I worked.

I did the chopping and cleaning while Dad did the batter.

He'd lost a lot of weight over the last while and he was drinking too much but he was cheerful and everybody liked him.

Since I'd been sort of full-time we'd been getting on great.

He had all these stories he kept telling over and over with little exaggerations getting worse all the time. But I never got tired of them.

Just before twelve, he'd have his first small one of the day.

He said it helped his blood flow more easily.

I'd gotten used to it, but sometimes I felt it was a bit early.

Because he'd have a couple with his dinner, and from teatime on, he'd sort of be topping it up.

That Friday I opened up a bit late.

People came in from about half.

I took orders in our sit-down part and Dad would put them on the counter.

I was like a waiter and the people knew me. I'd chat with them. Have a laugh.

Mostly though, people took their food away.

Then, about two, Simple Simon came in with his nephew, Charlie Dunne.

I was pissed off because they went into the sit-down part.

Dad wiped his hands and told me to get behind the counter. And he went to deal with Simple Simon himself.

Simon was a local councillor and had the only bookies in the town.

Dad owed him a couple of grand.

He borrowed it when Mum died.

He should've gone to a bank or the Credit Union, but he'd owed Simple Simon money before from stupid bets.

And Simon used to let him off.

He knew Dad wasn't going anywhere and if it came down to it, Dad could always give him a share in the chipper.

So Dad, like a fucking gobshite, thought he had a special relationship.

As if friends could never let money upset them.

Well he was learning the hard way because now Simon was calling in the loan.

And it was killing my dad.

I knew one of the reasons he kept tinkering with the car was because he was wondering if anyone would buy it.

But it could only go for parts and he'd be lucky to get two hundred for it. Like very lucky.

And I hated Simple Simon because he knew exactly what he was doing.

It would break your heart to see Dad trying to butter him up and Simon playing the patient generous old uncle.

He was a miserable cunt.

He wanted a smoked cod and chips and his nephew Charlie wanted a quarter pounder with cheese, two battered sausages, chips, and bread and butter.

Simple Simon used to always introduce Charlie as 'My Sister's Boy'.

'This is Charlie, my sister's boy,' he used to say. I think he said it to reassure people that Charlie wasn't some sort of scientific experiment.

His head was too big but his face was tiny.

And his arms were too long so he always had his hands in his trouser pockets like he couldn't stop playing with himself.

I wanted to spit in their tea but Dad would've killed me.

When I brought their stuff over Simon was acting like me and him shared some big secret that we both found funny.

He was always offering me a job.

He told me his fingers were in lots of pies and there were fewer and fewer ways out of this town.

I pretended I'd love to take him up but told him that my dad needed me.

He told me to think about it and he squeezed my elbow.

Charlie asked me for 'Red Sauce', which the rest of us know as ketchup and it gave me an excuse to fuck off.

They stayed for ages.

Simon read *The Independent*.

And Charlie didn't do anything.

He just sat there with his hands in his pockets.

And he seemed perfectly fucking content just to do that.

It scared the shit out of me.

It must have been getting on for three when they left.

Dad ran out after them to say goodbye, wiping his hands like Simple Simon was going to check them.

Charlie nodded at me. I was fascinated by the size of his head so I nodded back.

To make him do it again.

Of course, they didn't pay and my dad shot me a look that said he didn't want to hear any shit from me.

And I think it was then that the mad plan started to form.

And once it started, I couldn't stop.

There was a big bloke with a beard used to come into Reynolds' the odd time.

The old lads always bought him drinks, but he wouldn't chat much.

Most people steered clear of him.

He'd only ever come in the chipper about nine, when it was quiet. And he was usually there on a Friday.

If it was me serving him, I'd have a cup of tea while he ate. We'd talk shit mostly, and I wouldn't say I knew him particularly well. But I had heard a few different stories about him, in Reynolds'.

Fran Ferris said he was a gunman from the North who'd escaped and they couldn't extradite him. Shamey Devereaux said he was an armed robber out on parole trying to stay out of trouble.

This could well have been a load of bollox and he might have worked in Super Value – but I have to admit, there was something about him. And as far as I knew, Reynolds' was the only place would even serve him.

That night, Ray called about eight and he was upstairs with Carmel and Dad.

Joe was in our room and it was a fairly safe bet he was having a wank.

Everyone thought he was great.

He was always studying.

The bloke with the beard came in about half nine.

He asked me for a fresh cod and chips.

I was wondering what type of person he was.

The only thing I definitely knew about him was that he liked fish.

He was reading his paper when I brought it over to him.

The place was empty.

My heart was banging away like the Peugeot.

I sat down opposite him.

'Listen,' I said, 'I may be barking up the wrong tree completely, but I want to ask you something.'

He kept on eating and didn't look at me.

'What is it?' he said.

'I need a gun.'

He took a sup of tea and then he put it down and said, 'What do you want it for?'

I ate one of his chips.

JOE

I spent the evening with Fergus and Noel.

We were mates since being kids.

They called for me and we had nowhere to go.

We went down to the rocks where the shipwreck was. The tide was out and we could see most of it.

We were never allowed to swim out near it because a boy got stuck in it one time and died. But that was back in the seventies and none of us knew him.

The story was that the ship was carrying guns for the IRA in 1920 or something and the captain was an English fellow who had fallen in love with a girl in the town.

And she was in the womens' IRA.

And she got him to bring the guns over in the night. But she was supposed to marry some farmer further up the coast. And he had found out and and he tipped off the Black and Tans. So they arrested the girl in her house and captured the IRA men who were going down the beach to get the guns.

But the girl knocked over an oil lamp in the house and there was a huge fire.

This warned the captain of the boat and he scuttled it.

He was drowned and because a British soldier died in the fire the girl was hung.

That was the story the old lads in Reynolds' used to say about it.

But Frank told me the boat belonged to a fisherman called Vinty Duggan who crashed it after drinking a bottle of Powers.

It was hard to know who to believe.

The town was full of spoofers.

Dad said he wouldn't get involved in the dispute because he was from Italy and it was none of his business.

He said that Irish people would rather make something up and if that's what they liked to do, then he had no problem.

When I told him he was forgetting I was Irish, he just told me to believe what I liked.

Or better still, make up my own spoof about the boat.

But I wasn't really bothered. I just liked looking at it. Lots of things could have been true, who knows?

Fergus and Noel were skulling rocks at the boat and I was having a piss in the sea and I saw the girl I fancied, Deborah Something, up on the promenade.

She was walking along with some bloke.

I felt shit.

We went down to the amusements.

There was only one game I really liked.

It was an old one with a big rifle and you shot at targets that went back into the distance. Even though they were just a few feet away. They just got smaller.

It was only 10p still, because no-one ever played it.

When I got home the chipper was closed.

Frank and Carmel and Ray and Dad were watching some film with lawyers and rain.

But only Carmel was really watching it.

The men were drinking and chatting.

I said goodnight and had a shower.

There were clean sheets on my bed and on Frank's. I looked at Frank's books.

He had lots of thrillers and westerns.

I liked his books because the sentences were always short.

The writers gave you the facts.

In school we did books where nobody said what they meant and you had to work out what everybody wanted.

I picked out a book with a black and silver cover.

I always read what the newspapers had said about the book.

Things like, 'You won't find better pace anywhere,' *Chicago Tribune.*

Or, 'I couldn't put it down. The quickfire dialogue and action set-pieces make this a winner,' *Los Angeles Times.*

These books knew how to be read.

They usually started with somebody looking at their watch.

'Jack Brannigan looked at his watch and quietly cursed . . . ' That type of thing.

They also had good sex bits.

Girls whose nipples went as hard as peach stones and their soft skin became covered in goosebumps.

The blokes all had big mickeys and they came quickly the first time.

The next was slow and leisurely.

I read fifty pages of this book.

The ex-cop was a drunk, but he was trying to stay sober.

He was looking for the daughter of a drug dealer who'd been kidnapped.

He knew the city.

But it was changing.

It was summer.

I went under the covers and curled up in the clean sheets.

I was an ex-cop. But I had good in me.

Justice. That kid I shot was an accident.

I woke up when Frank came in.

He was chuckling. I could smell the drink.

I liked Frank, I wanted to be like him.

'Hey Frank,' I said.

'What's the story, Joe?' he asked me.

He was always asking me what the story was. It was three in the morning.

I asked him if he was going to bed.

He just kept laughing.

He told me to go asleep. But I turned on the light. I wouldn't leave him alone 'til I knew what he was laughing at.

He told me he was going to hold up Simple Simon's bookies.

I asked him when. He said Monday.

And I just thought he was really pissed.

I lay down and I thought about Damien.

I wished it was Monday so I could see him.

I wanted to talk to him about something we were both interested in.

But I couldn't think what that was.

RAY

During the weekend, I drove around with Carmel. The weather picked up and we played tapes. That sort of thing.

I sometimes felt a bit guilty.

Carmel beside me in a light print dress and my mind wandering into different beds.

We stopped for lunch in Longford.

I watched Carmel talking.

She was intelligent.

Probably even more intelligent than me.

But I was together and worldly and she was innocent and trusting.

She had that nobility some people have about them. This showed me what I was and I thought it was a good thing our souls don't have smells.

Because mine would stink.

But at the same time I was proud.

I was getting away with it.

We decided to keep going for Galway and spend the night.

I liked it when a Galway station came on the radio. It was like coming to a new place where you knew nothing about the community. Where they were all used to this radio station I'd never heard.

Do you know what I mean?

No? Fine.

We went to the Great Southern.

I checked in while Carmel rang home.

That hotel smell.

Dinner was from seven.

We went to our room. Thick carpet and a big bed. We swam in the deserted pool.

The chlorine in the air when we got dressed.

We had a few pints in the plush bar and made our way leisurely for a late meal.

If Carmel was unaccustomed to luxury, she didn't show it. She had assurance.

Which annoyed the fuck out of me.

We had a few more drinks. And we were too tired or too full to fuck.

And if you stay in a hotel, you've got to fuck.

So I made a point of waking up early.

We drove home Sunday.

I was refreshed and content.

After dropping Carmel off I went for a few beers with Tony Reagan, our professor.

The famous philosopher, Wolfgang Konigsberg, was visiting our department that week.

He was only giving three lectures.

The department had agreed to this but I wanted the chance of a question and answer session where we could discuss his ideas. I knew I could have this guy on the ropes if I had the opportunity to press him, not that I was particularly interested in his area.

Tony said we could talk about it, next day, at the Monday morning staff meeting.

That night I slept the sleep of the just and righteous and all that kind of shit.

The next morning I sat in my office looking at all my beautiful books.

Sometimes I'd go to the library late at night and just sit in between the shelves. Breathing in all those years of useless discussion.

I was working on a book I knew no-one was going to read.

What would be the point?

My office was on a corner of the highest part of the college.

This tickled Tony Reagan no end.

He said that the philosophy department was near heaven so that when the questions became too unbearable we could lean out the window and ask God.

Poor Tony was a terrible gobshite.

I sorted out two lectures I wasn't looking forward to giving that afternoon and I went to the staff meeting.

Tony Reagan always wanted to please everyone.

The rationalists, the empiricists, me.

This was a pity because we were just a bunch of selfish children and it wasn't worth it.

He should have just treated us like shit and told us to get on with the philosophy.

But there you are.

The first argument was about who should pick Konigsberg up from the airport.

This took about half an hour.

Trish Meehan was the acknowledged expert on his work, but she was relatively new and Reagan wanted someone who'd represent the department better.

This turned into a squabble.

In the end, six of us were to be at the airport in three cars.

This was lunacy but I kept my mouth shut.

I was waiting for the big picture.

I knew I could fuck Konigsberg up.

Trish Meehan objected to him having to get involved in a discussion, because he was nearly ninety and would already be exhausted from his lectures.

But she was just being a contrary bollox because she knew no-one would touch her with a ten foot pole. She was taking it out on the world.

I ranted on and on about how undemocratic this was, not to mention the importance of discussion to the progress of ideas, blah blah de blah blah.

Well I might as well have hopped up on the table and taken a dump for all the good it did.

They won, I lost and I fucking hate losing.

The only thing I could salvage was the satisfaction of making Tony Reagan feel bad by pretending to be really upset.

I got up, threw everything into my briefcase, and said I didn't see the point in continuing the pursuit of truth and knowledge in these conditions and some other swine could corrupt the kids in my lectures that afternoon, because I certainly wouldn't.

I gave Trish Meehan the finger on the sly, and I stormed out, slamming the door.

Half day.

Lovely.

FRANK

I had never held one before and I was surprised at how heavy it was.

The barrel had been sawn in half and the wood in the stock was chipped and cracked.

He didn't give me any cartridges.

I asked him when he wanted it back but he just smiled and told me to get rid of it when I was finished.

He was going away and he told me to wish him luck. I did and off he went.

We weren't open yet.

I sat there with the bag at a table.

I thought I was going to have a heart attack. But I felt brilliant at the same time. It was like I could hear and see everything very clearly.

Like I could solve anything by thinking.

It was a feeling of power.

I put the gun upstairs and got on with my work.

Dad joked with me.

He wanted to know if I'd been drinking, I was in that good a mood.

But he was the one who'd had a drink.

He was under so much pressure.

His face was grey.

I hated looking at him in daylight.

His skin hung around him like a coat on a hook.

I thought the fucking eejit was great.

I was going to do something for him.

I waited 'til things eased off about half two. Dad was reading the paper.

I went upstairs and got my stuff.

I had cut eye holes in one of Joe's bobble hats. I'd cut the bobble off as well.

I was going to ask him if I could borrow one, but he was in a funny mood.

I had an old parka jacket and a pair of tracksuit bottoms.

I put the hat on and shoved the shotgun down my pants.

Then I ran down and out the back.

Dad never saw me.

I went across the yard and checked the street. No-one about.

I went left down to the sea-front and right past the few houses before Simple Simon's.

The street was deserted.

I pulled Joe's hat down over my face and I yanked the gun out.

I took a few deep breaths and walked straight in.

No-one noticed me at first.

Charlie was sitting on a stool watching the TV.

Tim Byrne, one of the clerks was reading the *Irish Independent* and picking his nose.

Two aulfellas were filling out a docket with a stubby pencil.

And the man himself, Simple Simon Mc Fucking Bollox, walked out from behind the counter with a cup of tea.

'Alright,' I said.

Simon dropped his cup and Charlie fell off the stool.

Tim Byrne put his hands up and the two aulfellas started arguing about the second horse in a treble.

It was easier than I thought it was going to be.

I got everyone to lie on the floor of the shop, then I locked the door.

I told Simple Simon to give me every penny in the place.

He said it wasn't much and it wouldn't be worth my while.

He kept calling me 'Son'.

I pulled him up and stuck the gun between his legs.

He went white and did a shit in his pants.

I was smiling behind the hat.

He was telling me to take it easy.

I let him go and he sort of waddled behind the counter.

I jumped up on it so I could watch him and keep an eye on the others.

He pulled about thirty quid out of the till and I took it.

Then I said, 'And the safe.' I didn't even know if he had a safe.

But sure enough, he nearly started to cry and went towards the office.

'Leave the door open,' I told him.

He was kneeling on the floor.

Charlie was glaring up at me with his little piggy eyes.

I was terrified of him. But he just lay there.

Then Simon came back out with two big envelopes.

I leapt off the counter and stuck them in my pockets.

Then I told Simon to take his clothes off.

Naturally, he refused.

But I stuck the gun under his chin and he slowly unbuttoned his pants.

He was shaking so much I thought he was going to have a fit.

I nearly felt sorry for him, standing there with his tits like a girl.

I took him by the hair and we went to the door. I undid the latch and made sure there was no-one around.

I waited for a car to turn the corner at Reynolds' and I pulled Simon out with me and slammed the door behind us.

I could hear him thumping and shouting to be let back in. And I was around the corner like a shot.

I ran through the yard at the back of the bookies and over to the wall that adjoins the lane. There was a bin and I used it to get up and grab the top of the wall.

And then I nearly collapsed when I heard someone shouting.

Charlie was running towards me.

I fucked the gun over the wall and threw my leg up.

I caught my heel at the top and heaved myself over. The ground was lower on the far side and I fell in a heap.

I could hear Charlie getting up on the bin. I shoved the gun into my pants and started running down the lane.

I pulled Joe's hat off and the gun slipped down my leg. I grabbed it and limped past the back of Creevan's butchers.

I got out on to Main Street and headed for Super Value.

I had to get in somewhere before Charlie came out of the lane.

I could have gone into Mary Kennedy's pub but I never drank there and they'd have been talking about the time I came in for years.

It was too suspicious.

I was trying to walk normally and breathe slowly. Nobody paid me any heed.

But Super Value was too far away.

I was going to be caught.

And then Ray pulled over and gave me a lift.

Interval

JOE

That Sunday and Monday have to have been the two weirdest days of my life.

Frank didn't say anything about what he'd told me on Friday night, and to tell you the truth I'd forgotten about it.

I thought he was drunk.

Sunday started off normal enough.

Carmel was away with Ray, and Dad and Frank did the dinner.

They'd sort of taken over Mam's jobs about four years before, when she got really sick.

At the time I could remember her dinners and I knew that the new ones were different.

But now I couldn't remember.

I couldn't go to see her much.

I just couldn't.

One time she didn't know who I was and she got a fright when Dad told her.

She was roaring crying.

It was sick. I couldn't stand it.

I was glad when she died.

I had gotten used to her not being at home.

I didn't want to waste time getting upset. It wasn't my fault.

I didn't talk about her and I didn't like thinking about her. It scared me.

And that was all there was to it.

So anyway, after dinner on Sunday I was watching a brutal film and I was going to go up to my room, when the phone rang.

It was Damien.

There was a tickle in my stomach.

He wanted to know if I was going to Shadows.

It was a disco out near the dual carriageway.

Behind the Ancient Mariner bar.

I'd never been there and I knew my dad wouldn't let me go.

The Mariner was called the 'Bucket of Blood' because of all the fights and a barman had lost a finger once, trying to kick someone out.

Dad said it was full of gobshites and knackers.

Frank said that Shadows was crap and that the bouncers spent the whole night kicking people out, because they didn't refuse anyone. To get their money.

The bouncers would have to kick in the cubicle doors in the jacks and pull couples out who were having a quick shag.

But Frank hadn't gone there in years.

I told Damien I'd go if he was, but I had no I.D. and you had to be eighteen because there was a bar.

Damien said they never looked for I.D. if you looked anywhere near sixteen or so.

He asked me if I wanted him to get me some cans because he was going to the off licence. It was a good idea to get pissed before you went in, because the pints were £2.50.

I told him I wanted cans. But I didn't know how many to get.
I didn't know how many made you drunk.

I thought I'd aim high and told him to get me ten. He laughed and told me to stop messing. But I didn't know if that meant I should ask for more or less, so I asked how many he was getting.

He said four or five. I said to get me the same.

But then he said, 'What do you want?' And I said, 'Four.' And he said, 'Four what?' And I said, 'Four cans.' 'Of what?' he said.

I said Carlsberg. Advertising works.

We arranged to meet at the monument in the Christian Brothers' school where all the lunatics went.

I had to decide what to wear.

I had no good clothes.

In the end I took one of Frank's shirts.

It was black with a white pattern.

Little birds.

Actually I saw it again recently.

Stupid looking thing.

I had a shower and put on loads of talc.

I cut myself shaving, and when I put Frank's new aftershave on, my face went all red and angry. I looked like there was something wrong with me.

Which was unfair because I was right as rain.

I got my bike out and told Dad I was calling for Fergus and Noel.

The air was frosty and there was an orange glow over the city.

But out by us you could see the stars.

I knew Damien would be late because he always was.

I locked my bike at the bottom of the monument and went up about a hundred steps to where you could sit down.

It was a great view.

In the distance I could see Dublin Bay.

All the lights. It was very peaceful.

I thought about what my wife would be like.

But she just seemed to be like me and it got a bit boring.

After about half an hour, I saw Damien coming through the gates. He had a bag with him.

He was far away and very small.

I thought that if I'd had a gun I could have shot him.

I don't know what made me think that.

He was quite drunk already.

He sat beside me and I was asking him about Shadows.

He told me that if I didn't get my end away, he'd give me a hundred quid.

He had had a bottle of wine with his mum before coming out.

I thought that was great.

Then I thought about my mum.

She would never have drunk a bottle of wine with anyone.

I was a bit nervous about drinking the Carlsberg. I had had beer a few times at home and I'd liked it.

Dad put lemonade in it.

After two cans I'd felt happier than I'd ever felt. I was in love with Damien – in a friendly way.

I wanted him to myself, if that's what love is.

I couldn't finish my last can.

We went down to our bikes and we were laughing at nothing.

We wobbled all over the road.

There was a huge queue outside Shadows.

We were waiting for about twenty minutes.

The girls had mini-skirts or leggings but only a few had nice legs.

There was too much perfume everywhere.

It was in my mouth.

The blokes looked like they'd kill you as soon as look at you.

The bouncers wouldn't let a group of fellas in. They were barred.

They started shouting and saying the bouncers were fucking dead.

I couldn't see what the big deal was.

It looked like the sort of place I'd prefer to be barred from.

When we got in we were searched.

And we had to pay six fucking quid.

The music was brutal. I was made to put my jacket in the cloakroom, and I had to pay fifty pence.

There was pink fluorescent tubing all along the walls and around the dance floor.

I was trying not to catch anyone's eye in case I got a hiding.

Damien got a drink at the bar.

He knew some girls there.

I saw him dancing.

The place got packed really quickly.

I was getting tired.

I walked around and watched everything.

There was a stool at the bar so I sat there.

But then I had to buy a drink.

I got a pint of Carlsberg.

It made me feel better.

I saw a bloke who was about twenty.

He looked like he did weights.

He was on his own dancing at the bar.

He was on something.

A girl came over to him and they started getting off. Then she got off with someone else. It was mad.

It was a shithole.

Everyone behaved like animals.

I had quite a lot of principles.

At about eleven Damien came over to me.

He was holding a girl around the waist.

She was thin and she had dyed blonde hair.

She was smiling but she was very drunk.

Damien asked if I was ready to go.

Too fucking right I was, I told him.

He laughed.

He brought the girl out with us.

He was getting off with her while I unlocked the bikes.

She wanted us to walk her home.

She lived up near the Grange where all the knackers lived.

We walked down the dual carriageway.

They kept stopping and kissing.

We turned up by the garden centre.

There was a lane that ran up along the side of a hill.

It was really dark but it was a short cut for the Grange.

We had to go up by the old church with no roof that everyone said was haunted.

Damien told me to hang on.

The girl was nearly asleep and he took her into the graveyard.

I just wanted to go home.

I waited a few minutes because I thought they were going to the toilet.

But I got pissed off and went in to get them.

I saw something moving on a grave.

I nearly shit myself because I thought it was something crawling out of the grave.

But it was worse.

Damien had his trousers down and the girl's legs were on either side of him, like they were broken.

Her neck was on the low rail around the grave and her head hung over the gravel.

Damien was pushing into her like he wanted to put her in the ground.

I ran straight back to my bike and cycled home.

I said goodnight and got sick in the bathroom.

I wondered if the girl knew what was happening to her. I wanted to hop on my bike and go back.

But it was too late. It was pointless.

I lay in bed and I dreamed.

I saw the girl, and I saw the girl I fancied, Deborah Something, and I saw another woman in a red dress with no shoes on.

She was laughing at herself.

I woke up at four in the morning.

I stood in the kitchen drinking juice.

The horrible thing was that what I saw made me sick to my stomach, but at the same time it was really turning me on.

And that upset me.

I was in bits all that Monday in school.

Damien never came in.

I had to see him.

I wanted him to tell me the girl had a great time and he saw her home.

I didn't want to hear anything else.

I couldn't concentrate on anything.

When I got home, Dad was reading the paper.

I didn't want to speak to anybody.

I went straight to my room.

Frank and Ray were sitting on my bed.

And all over Frank's bed was the biggest load of money I'd ever seen.

RAY

It was the most bizarre fucking situation.

Head-The-Ball was after doing an armed robbery. And I'd done the getaway.

He was going mad with excitement. And I have to admit, it was fairly catching.

I was glad when Joe found us in the room because it made Frank act a bit more responsibly.

He was very straight and told Joe everything.

Joe was annoyed.

He wasn't sure whether or not Frank was taking the piss. He just didn't want to believe it. But you could see he did.

And he was shitting himself.

And this was getting on Frank's nerves and he wanted to get out of the house.

I told him he should just get back to work and pretend everything was normal.

But Frank was going mad.

So I said we could go for a quick drive.

Frank hid the money under his bed.

He had a suitcase there where he kept bits and pieces.

He'd gotten nearly thirty grand.

He made Joe come with us to make sure he didn't do anything stupid, and then we couldn't resist it, we drove by the bookies.

There were two squad cars parked outside and a guard was standing in the doorway.

A group of women had come out of their houses and they had their arms folded, talking about it.

It had only taken Frank about five minutes and he was sure no-one had seen him.

No-one was going to believe he'd done it anyway.

He kept telling it over and over and turning the radio on and off.

Joe was quiet at first, but then he started asking questions.

We drove along the coast.

Frank and Joe started to laugh at the whole thing.

Lunatics. But we all had different natures.

For now I was happy to roll along merrily and not get to upset.

I don't get upset much.

But the more Joe was asking what we should do next, the more I was beginning to see what a good fucking question it was.

I have that sort of philosophical training.

So after driving around for a while I decided that enough was enough.

It was getting a bit stupid.

I pulled over and told them what to do.

Absolutely nothing.

They had to go back and pretend nothing had happened. Listen to what people said, what the local theories were, and cultivate them.

They had to see which way the cookie bounced.

The last thing they wanted to do was a Thelma and Louise job.

Only a stupid prick would take off.

In a way, I wanted them off my back.

I didn't need the hassle.

So we went back to the chipper, and of course, I was right.

There wasn't a stir in the place.

Why would there be?

No guards had come. No nothing.

I had a bite with Joe and Frank got back to work.

People were coming in for their tea and asking Frank if he'd heard about the bookies.

And Frank was all, 'Yeah, what happened exactly?'

And the stories were all different.

Someone said it was a gang of raiders who'd gotten away in a car.

Someone else said the robbers had a stick of dynamite and they'd threatened to blow up the safe if McCurdie didn't open it.

Some fucking eejit with a woolly hat said a shot had been fired into the ceiling and the guards were looking for fingerprints on the bullet.

Joe was laughing but Frank kept a straight face. And I knew he'd be okay.

And later on when Carmel came home, we went up to her room.

What a beautiful girl she was.

What a fit girl.

Well.

In the morning there was a message on my machine from Tony Reagan.

He wanted to apologise for what had happened at the staff meeting.

He hoped I understood that it was Konigsberg who'd insisted on giving his papers with no discussion.

There was very little Tony could do but he would try to have a word.

I rang him back. I was gracious and I told him not to worry.

When I got into my office there was a note slipped under the door.

It was from the third year I'd slept with. She had wanted to meet me the night before. Well, too late now.

I fucked it in the bin.

I didn't have her in any classes that week and I'm going to be completely frank with you here. I didn't really like her.

And I have the guts to admit that, you know?

I took out the two books of collected papers I had by Konigsberg.

He had been developing this brutal theory since the fifties.

He said that language was an organic thing, like any plant or animal. And just like any plant or animal, it was born, lived healthily for a while, making other little languages, like its offspring, and then it died. Same as everything else.

And our language is dying now.

No-one talks properly.

There is a lack of sincerity, he claimed, because language is sick now.

It isn't vital enough to sustain validity.

Politicians are elected on saying the right thing strategically, not morally.

People in general aren't reading.

The action movie has replaced poetry.

People can't make an effort to be entertained.

They take drugs instead.

Blah, blah, blah, language is dying.

Now this meant that Konigsberg was either very clever or very lucky.

Because it made him hard to categorise.

He was a sort of Aristotelian, Darwinian, Marxist, Communitarian type thing.

And I don't know how much money he'd made hawking this notion around the lecture circuit. But I'd say it would have to be something pretty fucking amazing.

Tony Reagan knocked in to see me.

He'd just been on to Konigsberg's personal secretary or agent, or whatever she was.

And lo and behold, he had agreed to a very brief question and answer session after his last lecture.

I told Tony I owed him one.

But he said he was looking forward to it.

It'd be entertaining to say the least.

But I knew if I could nail Konigsberg, they'd be writing articles about me for years.

When he finally arrived, there was a big buzz in the college.

You see, nearly every department found him relevant, literature, linguistics, history, philosophy, everybody.

They had his first lecture in the evening so all the students would get a chance to see him.

He was in the largest lecture theatre but it was so full they had to rig up a closed circuit system to the next theatre, where everyone could see him on a huge screen.

With the question and answer session not happening 'til the third lecture I wasn't bothered going to the first two.

Anyway the thought of watching all those morons slobbering all over Konigsberg annoyed me.

And it made me jealous. I admit it.

It did.

There was a sort of reception thing after each lecture, which I did go to.

There was free wine and sandwiches.

Konigsberg was never there.

He needed his rest. Only post-graduates were supposed to be at these receptions and there were academics from all over Europe there especially.

But a bunch of philosophy students who were in with the department always blagged their way in to get locked.

So you had to be quick.

I got completely rat-arsed and all around me twits tried to be clever and funny.

I made a point of getting into a row and left. On the way home I phoned Frank to get the lowdown.

Everything was cool.

People saw the robbery as one of those things that happen, and that's life and it was a learning experience and that was that.

But at the same time, Frank was nervous and excited and he wanted to do something.

He wanted to unwind. He wanted to get away.

I didn't want him doing anything thick so I told him we could drive down the country at the weekend. Me, him and Joe.

That way I could keep an eye on them.

Konigsberg's last lecture was on Friday morning and I arranged to pick them up after that.

That was the plan.

On Thursday night, I was at another wine and shite-talk reception.

A bottle and a half into the proceedings and I spot the third-year chick.

And she was pretending not to see me.

I ask you.

And may God forgive me, but with every glass of Earnest and Julio Gallo, her tits were getting more imperative.

So I fucked over to the student bar with her and her bunch of know-it-all shitbrain friends.

And there we are, pint after pint and she's sitting beside me with her great big legs in knee-high boots.

And I'm getting a dirty mind and I know that if I don't get it in her in the next few minutes, I'm going to give someone a dig.

So we split and I'm giving her a lift home.

And her hand is down my pants and I open them up and Jesus Christ, she's sucking me like a starving baby.

So we get to her place, I'm fucked.

She carries me up the stairs into her room.

And I remember I was really interested in her keeping her boots on.

And I was just pulling off her knickers and the door burst open.

And this little fellow with long hair ran in, going berserk.

He jumped on me and she was shouting, 'Vyvyan, No!' He pushes me out into the landing.

I was trying to pull my pants up, and I fell down the stairs on to the hall table.

The phone flew off and went through the glass in the front door.

And I needn't tell you, I was out into the car like a bullet.

I locked my door and your man was banging on the roof. I reversed at about fifty miles an hour. I didn't even look.

I skidded across the street and got it into first. Vyvyan jumps in front of the car.

I put the foot down.

I'm not sure, but I think I might have clipped him. I wasn't going back to check.

I had a big day in the morning.

I was getting an early night.

When I got home I threw some stuff into a bag for going away with the boys.

Then I lay in the bath and I was dreaming about Martha Nussbaum.

We were talking about Aristotle and getting ready to go to bed for a shag and she lifted up her dress and she had a dick.

I jumped and woke up.

It was nearly two o'clock in the morning and the bath was freezing.

I poured myself a large glass of medicinal brandy, went to bed and shivered myself to sleep.

The alarm went off.

Ten o'clock.

Konigsberg's lecture was at eleven.

And Jesus Christ, early night or not, after all the wine and beer and brandy, not to mention lying in a cold bath for half the night, I was completely bolloxed.

I had an hour, but I could hardly fucking move.

I had a shower and a shave.

Tried to have a shit but nothing was happening.

I was in bits.

On the way into college I stopped for petrol and got some Solphadene and juice.

I put the carton to my mouth and I swear to God I couldn't stop drinking until the entire litre was gone. I was that dehydrated.

The lecture theatre was full of nobodies all out for as much enlightenment as their little heads could handle.

And there he was.

Professor Wolfgang Konigsberg was about five foot and completely bald.

He sounded like Spike Milligan doing Hitler impressions. I could hardly hear what he was saying.

It was giving me a headache.

Everyone was watching him intently.

Some were even nodding in agreement, going, 'Mmm, mmm.'

It would make you sick.

The third year chick was looking over at me. She was sobbing into a little piece of toilet roll.

I was beginning to feel worse.

There a gurgling sound coming from my stomach. There were waves of nausea.

I was sweating but my feet were freezing.

I closed my eyes.

Then there was applause and I heard Tony Reagan say, 'Professor Konigsberg has very kindly agreed to take one or two questions. And I know that Dr. Raymond Sullivan would like to ask the first one.'

That was me.

My eyes were watering.

My head felt lighter than my body.

And I was sitting in the middle of a row.

I couldn't get out.

Everyone looked at me expectantly.

Konigsberg was looking around, wondering who was going to say something.

And then, absolutely beyond my control, a long stream of orange puke shot out of my mouth.

It sailed across the room and all over the people for about ten feet in front of me.

I spluttered for a moment, and coughed a little, and then there was complete silence.

I immediately felt much better.

I wiped my face and looked around.

No-one could believe what they had just seen.

I stood up and cleared my throat.

'Yes. Thank you, Professor Reagan,' I said. 'I would like to ask Professor Konigsberg if, during his long and eminent career, he has ever seen anything quite like that.'

Tony Reagan didn't know what to do.

He just looked at Konigsberg.

The smell of sick was rising through the room.

Konigsberg didn't say anything.

And then, finally, he slowly shook his head.

I thanked him politely and made my way out.

I couldn't even remember what I had wanted to say.

Fuck it.

FRANK (*to Ray*)

I never heard that.

RAY

I've been saving it.

FRANK

It was a weird feeling.

I had thirty thousand pounds under my bed.

The first thing I did, the evening of the robbery, was bury the gun.

I took it up to the hill before the Grange and dug a hole under a tree in the woods.

I wasn't sure what to do with the money though. I didn't want to bury it in case it was too hard to get when I needed it.

And I was afraid to lodge it in case some case I knew at the bank got suspicious.

I was even afraid to look at it.

So it just lay there under the bed.

But no-one was on to me and that was obvious.

About the Wednesday, Simple Simon and Charlie came in for their lunch.

They were very quiet.

They'd lost their swagger.

I was a smart arse.

I was all, 'Do you think they'll catch whoever did it, Mr. McCurdie?'

And he was, 'I don't honestly think so, Frank, I really don't.'

Charlie couldn't understand how the robber had disappeared after running down the lane.

'I nearly had the bastard, Frank,' he said. 'I was about as close to him as I am to you now.' Which was too fucking true.

Simon was telling Charlie not to blame himself. There was nothing he could have done. And I was agreeing with them.

But I was sick to the gills when I thought about how lucky I'd been.

If Ray hadn't come I was fucked.

And what good had it done?

How could I pay Dad's loan off?

Everyone would know it was me.

I was getting restless.

Joe was moping around in the dumps all the time and I couldn't cheer him up.

I was hoping it wasn't my fault.

But sometimes you have to decide that principles will only fuck you up, because no-one else is ever moral.

I wanted to give Joe some cash.

I didn't know what I wanted.

When we were in bed one night, I said I hoped he wasn't angry at me.

But he wasn't.

He told me about seeing some eejit from his school having it off with a knacker from the Grange. It had really upset him.

But I couldn't see the big deal and I didn't know what to say to him.

I was annoyed at him.

But then that night I was thinking about a woman I knew when I was Joe's age.

I used to wash her windows and cut the grass.

She had two young children and her husband was a plumber.

I sometimes used to walk with her to collect her kids from school.

And then one day, in her kitchen, she touched my hand and I never went back.

I was going to tell Joe this, but he was asleep. I didn't see what it had to do with him anyway.

I decided we should get away for a few days.

I asked Ray. His car would give us that aimless millionaire feeling I was after.

I told Carmel I wanted her to work with Dad for the weekend.

She went bananas because she had an exam coming up. But I told her that Joe needed a break from his studying and she could be a Christian for five minutes.

That got her. She was guilty about Joe not having a mother, and she was always fighting with him.

I know it was mean, but she felt it and you've got to use what you've got.

I waited until Dad was into the second half of the bottle before I said anything.

He smiled. He thought it was a good idea.

What a great man. He made me proud.

I couldn't leave the money under the bed for the weekend. So me and Joe put it all into plastic bags with some stones, then we sealed them with elastic bands and put them in the tank up in the attic.

And when we came back down, it hit us that we should have taken some out for the weekend. We got all giggly and we were wondering how much we should take.

We didn't know, so we guessed on five grand.

Joe was cheering up.

I told him not to go into school on Friday because Ray would be picking us up at lunchtime.

In the morning I was washing the floor and the old man came over and handed me fifty quid. Of course, I was saying, 'No, no.' But he wouldn't take it back. 'For a drink,' he kept saying, 'Buy a round.' Then he winked at me and walked off.

It was the first time I'd felt guilty.

That man had done everything by the rules in his life and look what happened.

He was left on his own and shagged by bastards like McCurdie.

But he was right. That was the thing.

Well I didn't want to be right any more.

That's a load of meaningless toss.

I was glad when Ray showed up.

He looked like shit.

He was having a whiskey with Dad while I went to get changed.

Joe came in and told me Dad had given him twenty quid. He felt really guilty as well.

We broke our shit laughing.

We put the gear in the car and we were trying to decide where to go.

We hadn't thought about it.

Joe just said, 'Cork,' and that was it.

We were off.

It felt good to be moving.

We were taking the piss out of Marian Finucane on the radio.

They were going on about planning permission for sheds and extensions.

Ray said he'd give her shed an extension if she didn't shut the fuck up.

He had it in for everybody.

He was in bad humour because he was hungover.

So we stopped in Abbeyleix for a cure.

I wasn't sure how to treat Joe in this respect. But he just asked us what we wanted and bought the first round.

I was relieved.

The last thing I wanted was to have to be his parent. He had to grow up. Let him.

It was very nice there and we didn't want to go. But Cork it was and off we went.

I asked Ray which was the most expensive hotel. We could afford it.

Me and Joe shared a room.

Old habits.

And Ray got himself a double room, because, as he put it, you never know.

Joe was having a bath and I took Ray aside to give him a grand for the weekend.

He didn't want it, but I made him take it. We were like children playing.

We had a drink sent up to the room and Ray toasted me.

He said I was the weirdest bastard he'd ever met.

At nine we went down and had a beautiful dinner. We got champagne, but only Ray liked it. Me and Joe thought it was horrible.

Ray said we were the typical nouveau riche, all money and no taste.

Fuck him. We had pints.

Afterwards we headed into town.

Most of the pubs were packed but we found a little aulfellas' place that served us 'til about half twelve.

Back at the hotel there was a disco.

We got a drink and Ray started talking to a girl around Joe's age, and I don't know what he said to her, maybe he paid her, I don't know. But she came over, asked Joe to dance and got off with him the whole evening.

Joe was beaming when we went to bed.

But then he said he missed her.

Everything backfires.

You can't do fucking anything.

And that was what the weekend was like.

We were the boys.

Rested and refreshed.

Until we got back on Sunday evening and there was a squad car outside the chipper.

JOE

When we saw the guards, I think we all had the same idea.

To put the foot down and get out of there.

But it was too late. They saw us.

It was horrible.

Ray pulled over and a sergeant asked us to come in.

There was a detective sitting with Dad in the front room. Dad looked wrecked.

Carmel glared at us.

Frank was white and his hands were shaking.

But we were all completely wrong.

Because it was me the detective wanted to talk to. He asked me if I knew a girl called Sarah Comisky.

I didn't, I'd never heard the name.

Then he asked me if I ever went to Shadows nightclub.

I looked at Dad, but I had to say yes.

He asked was I there the previous Sunday.

I said I was and he nodded.

He just wanted to talk to me and Dad.

Everyone else had to go.

And when they were gone, he said I'd been accused of raping Sarah Comisky.

I nearly fell on the floor.

I said it wasn't me.

I didn't know any Sarahs.

But the detective told me to relax.

The girl hadn't accused me.

Damien had.

She had been attacked up in the graveyard near the Grange.

She had identified Damien as her attacker, but he said it was me.

The girl was very drunk but she did remember someone else being there.

So the guards wanted to find out if both of us had done it, or if one, which one.

Dad came with me down to the station and I had to give my account of what had happened. They made sure I got all the details right and then they gave me a cup of tea and a Kitkat.

Then Dad signed something, then I did and they took a blood test.

Then we could go home.

I couldn't believe Damien had dropped me in it like that.

But Dad said I was too naive and that people would do anything to save their skin.

He said he knew it was disappointing but that was the way it was.

At home we all sat up late and talked about it and everyone was great.

We all drank beer until very late in the morning.

In bed that night I thought about my mother. It wasn't about the times when she couldn't talk and gave me nightmares.

It was about another time I'd forgotten.

Dad was teaching me how to skim stones on the beach. And Mum was trying to do it and she couldn't.

It was summer and she had a red dress on.

Dad was slagging her and she was laughing at herself.

And I felt safe and the safe feeling stayed.

I didn't go to school that week and the guards called on Tuesday to say that my test was negative.

They were charging Damien.

There was a bit of a shindig in the house.

Frank told me he was putting money away for me to go to college, but I wasn't to say anything to Dad.

And Frank went to Chicago a few weeks later and he sent money back for Dad to pay off his loan.

Maybe he had a job, maybe he didn't.

Dad wasn't to know.

Ray brought a book out which nobody read.

But he was pleased.

He said that that was the point.

So in the end it was like things started off good, and just got better.

Is that cheating?

I don't know.

It's hard to say.

I can still see the girl.